Church Politics
and
Education in Canada

The P.E.I. Experience

Frank MacKinnon

Detselig Enterprises
Calgary, Alberta, Canada

Church Politics and Education in Canada: The PEI Experience
© 1995 Frank MacKinnon

Canadian Cataloguing in Publication Data
MacKinnon, Frank, 1919-
    Church politics and education in Canada

    Includes index.
    ISBN 1-55059-104-5
    1. University of Prince Edward Island--History. 2.
Education, Higher--Prince Edward Island--History. 3.
Catholic Church--Prince Edward Island--Political activity.
4. Church and college--Prince Edward Island--History. 5. Prince
Edward Island--Politics and government. I. Title.
LA418.P7M32 1995378.717'09C95-910269-8

Publisher's Data

Detselig Enterprises Ltd.
210, 1220 Kensington Road, NW
Calgary, Alberta T2N 3P5

Detselig Enterprises Ltd. appreciates the financial support for our 1995
publishing program, provided by the Department of Canadian Heritage,
Canada Council and the Alberta Foundation for the Arts, a beneficiary of the
Lottery Fund of the Government of Alberta.

Cover Design by Bill Matheson

Printed in Canada   ISBN 1-55059-104-5   SAN 115-0324

"I have always been strongly opposed to using religion as a gimmick for gaining political support . . . not only is patriotism the last refuge of the scoundrel, so is religion."

Rev. T.C. Douglas
provincial premier and federal M.P.

"Let me speak to the yet unknowing world how these things came about . . . lest more mischance, on plots and errors happen."

Horatio, *Hamlet*

*This book is dedicated to the memory of
Prince of Wales College, Charlottetown and
those who taught and studied there.*

Contents

Preface

"Church and state" is not an accurate synonym for religion and government. In practice there are *three* elements – religion, church politics, and government, a combination which is potent and volatile throughout the world. I had unique experience with these elements on Prince Edward Island where local churchmen handled them with extremes of apathy and aggression. They made this book inevitable, provided its plots and invited its conclusions. I present it as a constructive response to extraordinary events.

The Island reflects some national aspects of church politics. It has perennial problems with big government in a small place. Canada's troubles are now so serious her break-up is possible. The main difficulty is not "the system," which is good by any comparison, but bad management of the system, and a practice of hiding or enshrining mistakes which prevents reform.

These difficulties include church politics. Canadians debate other features of their crises, but not this one, which is mostly conducted in secret and almost taboo to discuss. It too needs open discussion and change if religion and government are to flourish in Canada and her provinces.

F.M.

Chapter One

INTRODUCTION:
THE SETTING

Religion is the highest expression of love; yet church politics often provokes man's inhumanity to man. They are different. Religion is the service and worship of God and love among His people. Church politics involve relationships, powers, business, and tactics in church affairs and between churches and other institutions. They can be in harmony or in conflict.

The world-wide failure and fatality rates of church politics are obvious, but they are rarely admitted by churchmen. Instead they are camouflaged with politicized theologies and theories of virtue and divine auspices. The result is what the Bishop of Durham called the "authenticity of spurious history." "All history," he says, "is made up, and church history is more made up than most."[1]

In Canada, fictional church history needs change in the interest of contemporary religion and government. Like any people, Canadians cannot build a distinguished nation or province on a foundation of spurious history.

This book presents a lively subject, the impact of church politics on higher education in Prince Edward Island. It includes a national dimension, so local issues can be examined in perspective, and because the story illustrates some of Canada's most persistent problems.

The forced union in 1968 of two colleges, Prince of Wales, publicly owned and non-denominational, and St. Dunstan's, church owned and Roman Catholic, followed two centuries of turbulent church-state politics that retarded the Island. What little is known of this story is mostly fiction. Clergy and laity gave full rein to fantasy; the local bishop issued an authoritarian political decree; government had ferocious rows in closed sessions. But the public was not given the facts. It is now my turn to speak for the record, as the last Principal of Prince of Wales.

Because the local diocese overwhelmed Cabinet and Legislature, a veil of silence descended. "Let sleeping dogs lie" became the official approach. But sleeping dogs have a nasty habit of waking up to bite when startled. And they do it again and again if permitted. With the past as a lesson and the future in mind, I therefore wish to protect the story from oblivion. The Island and the memories of Prince of Wales and its splendid service deserve no less. This is not a history of the College. It is not anti-religious or anti-any particular religion. Indeed, it is not about religion at all. It is a description of church politics with evidence and examples.

Such study is beneficial to religion. People who prevent questions about their churches may be protecting only their church politics in the interests of absolutism. They may forget that the founders of their own denominations – Catholic, Protestant, and many others – at first based their theology and practice on open questioning of contemporary church establishments. When troubles came it was often because of a church policy of keeping clerical business "confidential," and not discussing sensitive issues in public, a tactic which did much harm to religion.

That is the serious side of the subject. As it appears on the wee Island, a humorous side is often presented as potentates abound, and issues are exaggerated on the small political stage. Gilbert and Sullivan sang of it:

Yet the duties are delightful and the privileges great;
But the privilege and pleasure
That we treasure beyond measure
Is to run on little errands for the Ministers of State.

When little errands meet church politics anything can happen; and it does!

Tiny Prince Edward Island has one of the largest systems of governmental and church politics for its size in the world. A beautiful place with many assets, it is the little brother of a complicated federation in a sparsely populated half-continent. It is therefore guaranteed an active public life, and politics is its favorite sport. The Island's society was modelled on the French and British colonial systems in much larger places. Yet, even today, there has been no real adjustment of its state and church systems to only 125 000 people in an area 225 kilometres long and from 5 to 55 kilometres wide. The system operates like a 50 horsepower engine in a 10 horsepower boat – exhilarating, but dangerous.

The Island is a useful place in which to study priests, parsons, and politicians. Like a scientific model, it can aid research on larger systems by illustrating ideas and actions on a small scale. "Human nature," said Agatha Christie, who wrote on life and crime in little places, "is much the same in a village as anywhere, only one has opportunities and leisure for seeing it at close quarters."[2] And Marshal McLuhan featured the "global village." In an issue on world disasters, *Time* declared that "those who glorify the global village may not know much about the behavior of people in villages. Sometimes, as Cervantes understood, 'there is more harm in a village than is dreamt of.'" And, "the global village has no police force. What [it] does have is many churches. Sometimes it is the faithful of the churches, and the mosques, who need policing most of all."[3]

Prince Edward Island has long been an example of this need. Its church politics often interfere with man's relations with his God and love of his fellows. And its college crisis had little to do with education and much with church politics. Inhabitants of small places are often the last to know they have such problems, when they cherish mythical beliefs and comfortable self-satisfactions. The result is a tale of mischief and fear of it in high places, and a warning of what the island province and Canada should reform if education and religion are to thrive.

Canadians have recently had some severe shocks about respected groups and institutions. While knowing many assets in their society, they are finding a dark side which they need to admit and do something about. In Saskatchewan, for example, Maggie Siggins said of her book *Revenge of the Land*, that she wanted to "paint a fresh picture of the opening of the West," one more truthful than "the butter churning cute little sawdust golden myth of our pioneers." The "upper crust in the new towns," she wrote, "were stewards of the grandiose churches. . . . Their children grew up with unrealistic delusions of grandeur. . . . For over a hundred years, malevolence, unrequited ambition, and greed stalked the land."[4]

"When we turn to study the daily lives of the people," wrote historian James Gray, "we discover [those] who were boisterously optimistic and fun-loving, generous, neighborly, and tolerant, and simultaneously funereally bitter, cruel and vengeful."[5] The Newfoundland scholar, David Anderson, put the subject bluntly: "It is true that nationalism and regionalism can provide a cover of respectability for nests of bigots, louts, and charlatans. Canada is awash with them today."[6]

Canadians recently heard much about this dark side when, for example, many clergymen made remarkable efforts to offer themselves as personal examples in criminal offences. But Prince Edward Islanders seem not to have discovered it yet, or are aware of "how the Island was really won and by whom" but are too cautious to talk about it. This caution led to over-politicization of higher education and the church-dominated business of the colleges.

The issue was not a quarrel between the colleges. St. Dunstan's was a seminary and a "mission college" of the diocese of Charlottetown under the control of its active chancellor, the Bishop. Prince of Wales was responsible to the public authorities of the province who would not dare disagree with the

Bishop. The issue was, therefore, between Prince of Wales and the Bishop – in Island affairs a most unequal contest!

Chapter Two

BACKGROUND: FROM PARIS
TO CHARLOTTETOWN

Prince Edward Island's colleges invite attention to their origins. Everything at the start of the province foreshadowed the union issue, which began about 1800 with much the same opinions and actions of its climax in 1968. Any Island study also involves scale and perspective, because localism in a small area needs comparison with other times and places. This chapter therefore presents turbulent beginnings in a unique setting.

There is a major problem; Island history, like that of Canada, is not dull, but it appears to be. By ignoring it, or rewriting it, people miss the entertaining mixture of comedy and tragedy in their public affairs. The chain of events was dramatic, but it was bogged down in contrived respectability and quickly forgotten. Villains flourished, but people kept quiet about them. Many citizens had splendid achievements, but they were relegated to "safe" nonentity, leaving a harmless writer of girls' stories as the only "name" in Island history generally recognizable today. Success and failure, therefore, are overlooked; lessons of experience go unlearned; the spirit of harmony and the spice of controversy are not understood; and the record seems too good to be true. The result appears drab, just as history in dull colors does in Canada as a whole. "Britain and the United States," wrote Conrad Black, "had the stars, we had worthies."[1]

If I were Bishop of Charlottetown, a portrait of Cardinal Richelieu would hang on my office wall. The French prelate and first minister of Louis XIV is perhaps the best known church politician in history, and he took a direct personal interest in the New World. He was an architect of French Canada's way of life because he forced his policies upon her affairs, from which they went to Acadia and Prince Edward Island. Were he alive today he would be delighted that the Island's college drama reflected his policies, tactics, and results.

The significance of the Cardinal is still great in Canadian and Island history, even though it rests in the dim background. This account of him by an interested party in the college issue may be thought "controversial." I should therefore cite some distinguished authorities who have already testified to the facts, and then tell the story as it was – problems, worthies, and all.

Richelieu is everywhere associated with two famous documents that are basic in French and Canadian government. These are the Edict of Nantes of 1598 which protected the civil rights of Protestants in a Roman Catholic country, and Louis XIV's revocation of the Edict in 1685. The French Catholic Church led by the Cardinal declared that the rights protected by the Edict could be enjoyed only within the church. Following Richelieu's death in 1642, prelates put enormous pressure for revocation on the French king to which he succumbed.

This well known dispute among Christians devastated France over many years. French Protestants, called Huguenots, suffered punishments, exile, compulsory conversion, and death at the hands of the church. The St. Bartholomew's Day massacre in 1572 is still a world-wide symbol of ferocity. The siege of La Rochelle, masterminded by Richelieu in 1627, killed two-thirds of its 25 000 inhabitants. Yet, despite such upheavals, the Cardinal insisted on the revocation rather than leave the Huguenots and their rights alone. France lost a host of its ablest people, and the resulting decline made way for war, revolution, and three centuries of unpredictable government under eight constitutions. Thus France paid a high price for church politics, while religion, with its service to God and love among people, played no obvious part.

These church politics coincided with the French regime in Canada where they were soon duplicated, and where the revocation of the Edict of Nantes became official policy. The future of Canada, Acadia, and Prince Edward Island was then mortgaged with a tragic violation of civil and religious rights that started and sustained many problems. It was a formidable prelude to the college question on the Island, and to the nation's constitutional troubles of the 1970s, '80s and '90s.

A Canadian French-born Huguenot theologian described this violation in 1985, the 300th anniversary of the revocation of the Edict of Nantes. "The first settlers in Canada were Huguenot," said a commemorative statement by Rev. Pierre Goldberger, Principal of the United Theological College of Montreal, "Henry IV . . . wanted to make Canada a Huguenot refuge . . . Generations of Protestants and Catholics lived in harmony in New France. This period ended with the revocation of 1685. Jesuits and soldiers arrived from France to enforce the new policy, and the Canadian Huguenots were forbidden to meet for worship, hold land or settle permanently. Huguenots moved to the United States or back to Europe . . . religious freedom did not return to French-speaking Quebec until 1959."[2]

By then it was too late. The results were unfortunate. "New France," wrote Stephen Leacock, "was little more than an outpost in the wilderness. . . . [W.L. Morton estimated the population as 200 residents in 1642.] Over all was the fostering care of Cardinal Richelieu, determined as Champlain had been, to make New France a settlement, not an outpost. But New France was misguided from the first . . . it lacked settlers. The Huguenots, defeated and exiled, would gladly have come but their entry was forbidden. Their energy and industry must seek another flag."[3]

"One of the most significant features of New France was that it was solidly Catholic . . . " reported Maurice Careless.[4] "It was orthodox; there were no heretics or questioners. . . . " Cardinal Richelieu prompted by Champlain wanted no difficulties with Huguenots, and "ordered that the colony should admit Catholics only; and henceforth New France was a Catholic preserve. The church's hold extended beyond religion to matters of government, to education, and to the land." Bishop Laval "insisted on a large share in shaping policies of government. The church also exercised power over men's minds through controlling teaching and the institutions of learning [and] carefully censored thought and reading for laymen."

For all these reasons the Edict of Nantes and the revocation deserve a prominent place in any collection of Canadian constitutional documents, and in any discussions of rights and freedoms in a democratic state.

Principal Goldberger presented a practical question for discussion. "Many have speculated," he said, "about what might have happened in Quebec if religious freedom had been retained from the start."[5] Fair answers are worth considering. Most of the Huguenots, who were an able people, would have stayed, to Canada's immediate benefit, and more would have immigrated. The Jesuits and soldiers would not have been needed; and the persecution and expulsion of Protestants could have been avoided to permit the colonies to develop as they should. And French would have become a free language and culture, drawing life from two French streams, rather than one restricted monopoly controlled by church politics. The "French fact" would be a fact, not a status, and a far stronger protection for the language and encouragement for French literature than the guarded policy of brittle political purity touted today.

Most important, however, was the likelihood of more sensible and Christian relationships among French and English and Catholics and Protestants. As Dr. Goldberger noted, French Catholics and French Protestants mixed well at first. Then the French Protestants were forced out by French Catholics and new ones were refused admission, leaving an exclusive French and Catholic monopoly to dominate the colonies and later Quebec. It was, therefore, French

Protestants who were oppressed by Catholic fellow Frenchmen, not French Catholics by the English as later alleged. Were they alive today, Henry IV and Louis XIV would no doubt remind us that Canada got Richelieu's church policy implemented as a governmental one. They might also admit that bilingualism and ecumenism would have worked in Canada if the Huguenots had remained.

Accordingly, Canada was to have, not a continuing French-English struggle as is commonly believed, but a Catholic-Protestant struggle disguised as a French-English one. It was an unequal contest when Quebec's society became Catholic by expelling French Protestants and forbidding their immigration, while "the rest of Canada" became mixed. Nothing is said publicly about this; but after the expulsion, church politics, not linguistic interests, had to dominate public issues. And, although Richelieu and the church directed the proceedings, religion itself obviously had no place in this political feud among Christians.

These politics invite comparison with Quebec's provincial language legislation today, the effects of the Charter of Rights, the exodus of English-speaking Quebecers, as well as changes of emphasis from bilingualism and biculturalism to francophone-anglophone relations, which are very different and which preserve the church interest with language at birth.

Richelieu's policies were implemented with skillful tactics among the few hundred colonists, by two extraordinary clerics who are now virtually unknown to Canadians, despite their impacts on public life. They are regarded as villains in history.

François Leclerc was one of the most famous of church politicians and a fixer of remarkable skill. Known everywhere as Father Joseph, he was the "Grey Eminence" of Cardinal Richelieu. Aldous Huxley's biography of Father Joseph indicated "a statesman, absorbed in the most dangerous kind of power politics and to all appearances quite indifferent to the appalling sufferings for which his policy was responsible."[6]

Corruption and bribery of opponents were handled deftly by Father Joseph for the Cardinal. He illustrated how simple it is to find and manipulate those who would betray a trust. "In Richelieu's enterprises," wrote the French scholar Gustave Fagniez, "treason was almost always called to supplement open force, or to make force unnecessary."[7] Under pressure many leaders deserted the Protestant cause, and "crossed over to the Catholic Church and became 'realists' . . . because the will to unity which their great enemy the Cardinal possessed was wanting among these Calvinistic individuals."

Father Joseph "employed the usual spiritual weapons . . . but when occasion demanded he supplemented these with other, more mundane forms of persuasion – the offer of gifts from the royal exchequer, pensions, honors, positions in the administration. Astute Protestant noblemen saw their chance and drove shrewd bargains."[8]

Later pages will illustrate these tactics as they were used in Charlottetown where they were examples of how "the will to unity" can be an ambition for monopoly control.

Richelieu's policies and Father Joseph's tactics went to Acadia and Prince Edward Island on the initiative of Abbé Jean-Louis LeLoutre. A Iago of intense villainy, he literally devoted his life to spreading ill-will in Canada and Acadia from 1737 to 1772. He became the "link between the French authorities and the colonists," says the *Canadian Encyclopedia*, and concerned himself with keeping Catholic colonists from accepting Protestant control, provoking Indians into annoying British colonists, and urging Acadians to leave. Indeed, the departure of the Acadians was not an "expulsion," but a manipulated exodus encouraged by LeLoutre and his church. He acted as a French, Quebec, and Catholic *agent provocateur* after the colonies became English. He would have been guillotined for treason had he worked for the English in a French colony. Despite his work being hindered by three prison terms, he continued to do much permanent damage and was conveniently forgotten.

Examples of Abbé LeLoutre's kind of tactics on the Island were described in a lecture in Charlottetown by an Acadian historian, Georges Arsenault, on the subject of Father Georges Antoine Belcourt. There were three issues: health problems resulting from too much intermarriage among Acadians; a suggested desire of Quebec and Paris authorities to "remove the whole of the Acadians from Prince Edward Island to Canada and there swell the numbers of the French-Canadian population;" and Father Belcourt's wish not "to take all Acadians from the Island because it would diminish the importance of the Catholic presence in the colony."[9] This remarkable story is an important neglected background for the old complaints and new aspirations of Acadians on the Island.

The Richelieu policies and tactics were followed by a political and ecclesiastical scramble before, during, and after the Seven Years War of 1756-1763. The events of those years were much less glamorous than what Canadians have been led to believe; and mistakes of the time remain to haunt the present. The true story has been well documented, but being controversial and difficult to live up to, it is hidden from public view by a jingoistic fairy tale.

The fairy tale is about benevolent mother countries, founding races and cultures, proud ancestors, the Canadian "we came over on the Mayflower" syndrome, and other pretensions. The real story gives Canada no "mother" countries, just a quarrelling pair of political great aunts, one of whom – France, disowned her, while the other – Britain, adopted her with reluctance. Exploiting a rich environment and chasing elusive political powers were much more popular activities than building a nation. Traces of "founding" and "cultures" were faint. One "race" only was involved among the white men. Date of arrival was no indication of deserved status: just being "here first" was not founding; and the Protestant French were among the "here first," but their status and rights were destroyed by Catholic fellow citizens. Indians were treated as badly by the newcomers as their tribes treated one another. The first settlers, like those of Australia, included many failures and felons unwanted at home, a fact recognized by Australians but not by Canadians; and soldiers and traders who came temporarily and stayed only because they could not get back to Europe. Still others who were successful colonists left for more hospitable places, or were pushed out in the prevailing rivalries.

No one wanted Canada then, and her real founders, who came long after discovery, were not the proponents of the fairy tale, but a more heroic breed of men and women – doers with hope and ambition – not whiners collecting chips for their shoulders. These credible pioneers overcame prevailing pessimism, hardship, and political intoxications, and changed their country from a nasty colony to a land of opportunity with world-wide respect. Unfortunately, their voices were muted in history and the fairy tale prevails.

On the local scene, Prince Edward Island was not developed by "founders" but misused by unbelievable incompetents. Indeed, Islanders who proudly look back at their family trees would be wise to stop at 1800. Before that time the colony was not regarded as a "fair Island of the sea," as its hymn calls it, but a costly nuisance to be fobbed off on absentee proprietors and given a government of its own to get it off other governments' hands. When the Island's real founders came later in the 1820s and 1830s they had a lamentable heritage to overcome.

The "great aunts" treated Canada and Acadia like unwanted foundlings. There was no Conquest, only a give-away, because France could have kept the colonies as Britain wanted her to after the end of the War in 1763, but she refused to take them and gave them away to Britain who did not want them either. There was no "planting firm Britannia's flag" because money was scarce after the war. The British government made a serious mistake when it took over by not restoring immediately and publicly the rights of the Edict of Nantes to French Canada, thus doubly protecting the French Protestants and serving much-needed notice to Abbé LeLoutre and his colleagues that both the tradition of French kings and British constitutionalism had replaced Richelieu's policy and new authorities were now in control. Alas, the opportunity was allowed to slip by and more chips were added to certain shoulders. With "peace" France continued to resent her defeat in a world war which began in Europe and had no relation to Canada. The battle on the Plains of Abraham was only one engagement in that distant contest, exaggerated in history to hide the give-away. France was allowed to wash her hands of the colonies, yet keep her fingers in their business and undermine Britain's efforts so that what little community spirit there was in the land rested on the flimsiest identities.

These identities were to continue flimsy through the next two centuries. It was hoped that cultural development would help, but it became so factional and politicized, it delayed the impact of a national culture. British cultural heritage encountered competition from the United States. The imported culture of France was used as a handy political and ecclesiastical weapon, and it was not sufficiently encouraged for its own value. No less an authority than the French Ministry of Culture spoke frankly: "The French were not as interested in culture as they like to think." "We French are an arrogant people, so what is important to us is to have the appearance of being cultural and not the fact."[10]

The Indians of Canada have today brought the whole subject of church politics in the New World into the open, and destroyed the traditional story of devoted missionaries carrying the faith to fortunate aborigines.

Saul Terry, president of the Union of B.C. Indian Chiefs, was one of many native leaders to speak on the subject. This group sought financial compensation "for the spiritual crimes and human rights violations committed by the Roman Catholic Church against our peoples ever since their missionaries first came into our territories." Chief J.J. Sark of the Maritime Micmacs made the same request to the Pope in a personal interview.[11] The Coalition of Concerned Canadian Catholics asked the Canadian Conference of Catholic Bishops to find "appropriate ways to express our repentance for the sins committed by the Catholic colonizers of the Americas."[12] The Catholic Coalition had distinguished evidence to back these requests. Alexander von Humboldt's biographer described the great explorer's opinion of the Spanish padres after visiting South America in 1800: "With their soul-hunting expeditions and their cruel treatment of aborigines, they emerge from Humboldt's travel accounts as the real savages. . . . Possibly the experience of seeing the symbol of the Cross wielded with the savageness of gun and whip accounts for Humboldt's disdain for organized religion."[13] There need be no surprise, therefore, at the punishment the Jesuits received from the natives, only astonishment that they were given the status of martyrs and the reward of sainthood by the church.

These accounts indicate the kind of atmosphere associated with Richelieu's policies as they went from Paris to Quebec, and eventually to Charlottetown. But, a cleric may ask, what about carrying the gospel to these new lands? The answer of one theologian explains the reaction of Humboldt and the Indians, as well as much of the indifference toward churches today. In Mexico and elsewhere, wrote J.V. Langmead Casserly of the General Theological Seminary of New York, "the religious conflicts and excesses of the sixteenth and seventeenth centuries did more than anything else to create a climate of cultivated opinion in which religion was not and could not be regarded as a proper subject of rational thought at all. The troubles of the world seemed very largely due to the irrational fanaticisms of religion."[14]

This statement is unfair to religion. It is church politics that are the problem.

But, the cleric may continue, why should churches not be involved in politics? This question, which goes far back to the days of shamans and medicine men, is answered in Frank G. Slaughter's biography of the Emperor Constantine, the modern church's Roman co-founder. The Emperor, he said, realized that "highly organized as it was through bishops, local churches and clergy, the Christian faith could help him unify the Empire." "By placing religion in an intimate relationship with secular affairs, Constantine undoubtedly laid the groundwork for the political difficulties that led to turmoil between church and state in later centuries and even to wars between nations."[15]

Thus did Christianity become what Edward Gibbon called an "independent and increasing state in the heart of the Roman Empire," a position it now occupies in Canada and Prince Edward Island.[16] Catholic treatment of the Canadian Huguenots and its results were part of this encroachment; and Canada has not recovered from the revocation of the Edict of Nantes.

This historical background does not just explain origins of issues. It also warns those involved with church politics as participants or observers that any action of Catholic authorities is based on centuries of continuing political experience. By contrast, Protestants operate in a succession of temporary situations with virtually no-one skilled in long-term policy and tactics. It is interesting to watch a group of mixed clergy and laymen discussing a major problem. One soon notes who is well briefed, and who is playing "blind man's buff."

Three centuries of experience suggest with ample evidence that Canada's political fairy tale does not deserve its dominant place in history. It has caused endless quarrelling among the people and much instability. It accounts for touches of a well-known inferiority complex in our public life. It is simply not working because it is not true. Had early Canadians been allowed to discuss it frankly, later generations would have been saved much turmoil, and if our generation does not speak up, descendants will bear the burden indefinitely and perhaps, as events warn now, lose Canada altogether because of it.

On Prince Edward Island, church politics and college history illustrate this Canadian problem. They suggest with startling clarity that, had some courageous discussion and action taken place in public right from the start, and had some chips been knocked off from time to time, the province would have avoided many failures, and achieved much success that was deserved over the years but thrown away.

Chapter Three

POLITICS AND THE COLLEGES

Britain's initial colonial policy for Prince Edward Island was to avoid costly responsibility and encourage settlement. There was little to start with in 1763 – only 271 isolated inhabitants. The Acadians had done nothing substantial with the place. New English immigrants were on the whole incompetent, and institutions were ramshackle. But there certainly was a big government, with a Governor, Lieutenant-Governor, Council, Supreme Court, and civil service, and provision for a legislature in the near future. Life on the Island soon became overwhelmingly political.[1]

There was not much by way of economics to support all the politics. As the 19th century approached, reported Professor J.M. Bumsted, the Island's economy "remained as it had been from the outset, agrarian and unspecialized," and was "conducted on barter principles or on credit. Holding public office was virtually the only way to assure a regular income, thus explaining the incredible attraction of office, however minor, to the inhabitants," as well as the tendency of those not on the civil list "to accumulate as many petty functions as possible." Indeed, he noted, "many critics of the government complained constantly of the menial origins of those who had risen to prominence."[2]

After about 30 years of slow development, facilities for advanced education became necessary and urgent. Industry, especially agriculture, required trained workers. Young people had been going to other places for advanced schooling, and often did not return. And one of the Island's perennial weaknesses – dependence on patronage – was holding back the recognition of personal qualifications. Successive Governors recommended the establishment of a college to local politicians and the Colonial Office. Governor Edmund Fanning personally gave the Island ten lots of land in 1804 for a campus. But much of this land was diverted to other purposes, church opposition delayed the project, and nothing was done for another three decades.

With the arrival of more competent settlers by the 1830s the need became urgent, and the new College was founded by royal charter of King William IV in 1834, under the name "The Central Academy." The Lieutenant-Governor was designated Patron and Visitor, and a Board of Trustees was appointed under the chairmanship of the Chief Justice. The Academy's name was changed to Prince of Wales College in 1860 in honor of a visit to the Island by the then Prince of Wales, later Edward VII. Another change in 1879 added to the College the separate Normal School which had been a badly-run fiasco.

This College was regarded by the authorities as the Island's great project in higher education. It was set up sensibly in relation to the expected student population and the scholastic requirements of the day. It was all the Island could be expected to afford and maintain. Expansion could happen later as the future required. Its reputation started early and progressed well, and its program was, and remained, the cornerstone of the provincial education system. It was publicly-owned and non-denominational from the start and throughout the years.

Nevertheless church politics on the Island obstructed a cohesive educational program by insisting on a second large administration that rivalled the government's. The Roman Catholic Church was, like the government, to have a big machine, which would be presided over by a relatively enormous swell, a bishop. The administration would bring with it the traditional ecclesiastical policies and tactics from Rome, Paris, and Quebec. Until 1829 the Island's Catholics were under the jurisdiction of the Bishop of Quebec and most of their priests came from that colony. Church politics thus slipped easily into the Island to stir up the Acadians with delusions of French colonialism at a time when this British colony was having trouble enough getting started.

Meanwhile, on the other side of the ecclesiastical fence there was no effective power at all. Like the Colonial Office in London, Protestant authorities, such as the Society for the Propagation of the Gospel, were unable to get enough good clergymen to go to Prince Edward Island, and too often sent incompetent ones with no future in the old country. This was also true of the priests, but for them there was a powerful bishop with direct personal control who was both a symbol and a boss. As for church laymen in public life, the Catholic ones could count on organized church support, the Protestant ones could not. And those dependent on votes in tiny constituencies, where every vote counted, were always vulnerable to both organized Catholic activists and Protestants of the "peace at any price" school of thought. The Protestants, indeed the whole society, were the losers, because those who seek peace at any price always pay an exorbitant price, or force others to pay it for them.

Any new Catholic bishop became the chief potentate in the colony as soon as he arrived, especially after the P.E.I. diocese was given a bishop of its own in 1829. He overwhelmed in status and power the Lieutenant-Governor and Premier, as well as any clergy in other churches. And he played to the hilt the role of "Grand Inquisitor." There was no more need for him among a few hundred Catholics than there was for an Anglican bishop; a monseignor would have been more appropriate, and healthier in what was hoped would become a legislative system of responsible government. The need for an Anglican bishop was discussed from time to time, even as late as the 1960s and 1980s, but the Anglicans passed up the opportunity of a balancing counterpart to Catholic episcopal power. They had to work through the absentee Bishop of Nova Scotia, while the ever-present Catholic bishop could make many decisions on the spot.[3]

The Island illustrated one of the most remarkable features of the struggle for responsible government in democratic societies. Freedom, independence, local responsibility, and severance from colonialism were the popular concepts in the Canadian colonies of the 1830s, and still are in many new countries around the world. Ties with mother countries were loosened, and newly-formed local governments assumed responsibilities with the electoral consent of representative legislatures. Anglicans everywhere gradually reduced the control of the Church of England in the colonies. But this change did not take place in Catholic affairs. No ties with Rome were severed; the Pope, an absolute monarch with the title "sovereign pontiff," remained the ultimate church authority. Because church politics were so great a part of Island politics, much public policy had been predetermined in Italy.

The churches did make one concession to responsible government by joining the party system. Four political party categories appeared early on the Island – Liberal, Conservative, Catholic, and Protestant – and they still remain.

As soon as the publicly-owned, non-denominational Prince of Wales College was founded Catholic clergy declared they would not support it, despite the fact that Catholic students attended it. They confused the theoretical principle of religion in education and the practical reality of church politics in education. The church wanted a second college of its own, despite the tiny and impoverished population, the shortage of funds for even one institution, and the obvious dangers of splitting the already small community into factions. With little of importance to do, an ambitious bishop must have found establishing a college an inviting personal project, as well as a means of separate identification and enhanced status for his small flock.

Two Catholic Colleges appeared. St. Andrew's in the village of that name was set up in 1831 and closed in 1844. St. Dunstan's College began in Charlottetown in 1855. Four conflicting policies were advocated in succession. One was the privilege – declared by its advocates to be a right – in which religious teaching was to be a major part of the Catholic institution. The second, put forth by supporters of public education, declared that young

Christians should not be so divided. When the second did not work a third policy was urged – that those wanting special treatment should pay for it. The fourth policy was that a church college should be financed by the state. It was not accepted at first, but, as in all provinces, it was the goal to which controversy was directed.

A fifth view was not a policy but an encouraged inclination. If Catholics had their own college why should they attend or support the state one? In support of their own, why not weaken the state one with active criticism and opposition to its funding? The state could not fight back, and Protestants would be labelled bigots if they did so, on the ridiculous assumption that their criticism would be more bigoted than the Catholics' action. Meanwhile nobody gave much support to still another idea, that other denominations might want the same separate institutions that the Catholics had.

The Island's historical records indicate that open and bitter hostility in church and public life lasted an incredible period, from 1763 to 1880! But the fight did not end; it went underground and kept on going. There is a long sad book to be written on this subject some day, and it is much needed because most Islanders know nothing about it, although it has been their biggest problem, preventing P.E.I. from developing as it should. But opposition to its publication and distribution would most likely be immense because, no doubt, politicians and clergy would be ashamed of what their predecessors did and censorship is active on the Island. Citizens would be shocked at the costly rivalry perpetuated by churches and passed on to them, and at what progress the Island could have made had public life not been saddled with church politics, its cost, and its divisiveness.

It is not surprising that much evidence was destroyed locally. Fortunately, archival activity increased in Ottawa about 1940 on the initiative of the Public Archives of Canada and the British Colonial Office. What Island papers they collected and preserved tell a remarkable story, and so do the surviving *Legislative Debates* and other official documents.

The story presents unedifying spectacles on glebe lands, official pews in churches, when bishops should be Irish or Scottish, church patronage, reading the scriptures in schools, incorporating the Orange Lodge, demands by French and Gaelic speakers for special examinations for their children, grants for St. Dunstan's and separate schools. Each side in the legislative debates thundered about the theology and worship of the other. The history of the papacy, the Protestant reformation, and the Orange Lodge were dissected in detail in the Legislature. No abuse was too scathing, and no revelation too personal on everything from which church's turn it was for some patronage, to allotment of funds, even to sexual peccadilloes of clergy. There were threats of physical violence. Hon. George Coles challenged Hon. W.H. Pope in the House – "I will meet you any day with sword and pistol."[4] It is not surprising that a special statute was passed entitled *An Act to prevent congregations being disturbed or disquieted during the performance of Public Worship.*[5] The climax of this behavior was spectacular. The election of 1876 returned an all-Protestant Liberal-Conservative government coalition, and an all-Catholic Conservative-Liberal opposition coalition.

The most striking fact about church political turmoil was its effects on religion. Its own supposed guardians stood in its way, and often were not good examples of its principles. All the church issues involved were not about the service and worship of God, not the alleged love of Christians for one another, but shabby squabbles based on cynical expediency. Politicized churchmen displayed jealously the "dog-in-the-manger" syndrome, to prevent others from performing some service or getting some credit. But the name of God was invoked to hide or justify this rivalry, the public was kept as uninformed as possible, and the mounting costs of church rivalry were literally never considered. Because the many mistakes were not admitted or examined, they remained the same from Richelieu's day to contemporary Prince Edward Island and its university issue.

In addition to the ill will, church politics took disproportionate amounts of time and money from the government that could have been devoted to developing the province and doing its business properly. It delayed the solution of other issues of the day, like the land question, railway building, and Confederation. It was an unnecessary barrier to cooperation among citizens. It was unjustifiably expensive, and drew funds from almost every enterprise, usually upon the threat of a row. Anyone who wishes to confirm this account needs only to look up the public documents and newspapers from the period 1763 to 1890. They will also see many examples of contemporary problems and will observe how vulnerable Prince of Wales College was to the antics on both sides in the Island's sectarian tragedy.

Having stated the problems and political atmosphere in a general way, we should consider difficulties of a practical kind.

On the power of the Bishop of Charlottetown, one continuing situation speaks eloquently. There were, for example, 15 governments and ten premiers in the 31 years from 1860 to 1891! In the same period there was one Catholic bishop, Peter McIntyre. Described in a Charlottetown newspaper in 1992 as having "reigned over" his diocese, Karen Kearney wrote, "he was a forceful, stubborn and energetic man, capable of dominating those around him, and of using politics and politicians to promote the rights and status of Island Catholics."[6] As far as can be determined, there has not been one Protestant clergyman or one Premier on the Island with such power and influence. Of all the 35 Premiers only two might be compared with the Bishop in a limited way – W.W. Sullivan, 1879-89, a Catholic, and J. Walter Jones, 1942-54, a Protestant.

What a powerful bishop can do is well known from, for example, the biographies of Bishop McIntyre's extraordinary British contemporary, Henry Cardinal Manning. Indeed, an understanding of the Island's bishops as church politicians can be secured in an entertaining and informative way by a comparison with Manning. He was a married Anglican Archdeacon who converted to Catholicism when his wife died, and soon became the Catholic Cardinal Archbishop of Westminster upon displacing the incumbent co-adjutor of Britain's senior see! He participated in everything from parish politics to Vatican affairs, became an influential adviser to Pope Pius IX, and was the sponsor of the doctrine of papal infallibility. A consummate politician in both church and public affairs, he was ambitious, ruthless, and dominating. He almost ruined the career of Cardinal Newman. Having McIntyre in Charlottetown was like being managed by Manning in Britain.

To me it is remarkable how episcopal grandees, with the whole Island for a diocese, could run St. Dunstan's and be allowed to meddle in Prince of Wales business and not be publicly questioned. Even more remarkable is how politicians and Protestant clergy let themselves be manipulated and silenced. An Anglican Archbishop or a Moderator in Canada enjoys no such privilege or immunity as the bishops on P.E.I. did.

Explanations came from St. Dunstan's itself, and were indicated in an interesting history of it by Professor G. Edward MacDonald published by St. Dunstan's in 1989.[7] One who reads this history may well believe that, had it been available to the public before 1968, the union of colleges would not have taken place. It indicates why the public college should not have been united with the denominational one, why it was a benefit to students to have a choice between two very different colleges and curriculums, and the fact that the two institutions had nothing in common.

The book shows that St. Dunstan's was never a university in practice; it had the title only, which was conferred by Bishop Henry O'Leary and confirmed by the Island Legislature in 1917 without appropriate investigation or discussion (pp. 36-38). St. Dunstan's was a seminary, and it was run like one right up to the union of the two colleges. It was prevented from becoming a real university by the Bishop, who controlled it personally as its Chancellor, and by its priests, who were parish clergymen alternating between manse and campus without appropriate academic experience. St. Dunstan's was so ecclesiastic that on its campus normal concepts of universities and the way they operate could have no place.

The illustrations in Professor MacDonald's history are devoted almost exclusively to priests. All the Island's bishops are the book's heroes, and it is indicated that they ran the college personally with a veto power over everything. St. Dunstan's was identified by the clergy as a training ground for priests, and Bishop Henry O'Leary was devoted to it as a "mission college." The author describes how, in 1880, the College was "placed under the control of the Jesuits, rather than closed," because "financially and administratively St. Dunstan's was a shambles." It was an arrangement that, because of the Jesuits' reluctance, was terminated by them a year later.

Professor MacDonald gives a long and clear description of the dominant church policy at St. Dunstan's. "Roman Catholicism permeated every aspect of College life." The Bishop had a veto power which he did not need to invoke because "his opinion invariably carried the day. . . . St. Dunstan's was envisioned as a diocesan institution designed to meet Catholic ends."[8] An alumnus remembered that an article written for the student magazine won a prize, but it was "rejected because of no religious content." Even when I went to Prince of Wales as principal in 1949, "the sense of community at St. Dunstan's was inextricably bound up with religion."[9] The situation was illustrated by a photograph of the faculty in 1948. It shows 20 professors of whom 14 were priests with backgrounds in parish work and six were laymen.

My chief complaint about the book is that everything in it is presented as "religious." However, much of its content describes what is purely political; the author's bishops come across as the wiliest politicians on Prince Edward Island. What influence St. Dunstan's had it owed entirely to the diocese of the same name. The faculty were presented as mostly parish priests. One looks in vain for a recognizable scholar, indeed an experienced university teacher among them, because their academic initiative and direction were so determined and confined by their priestly qualifications and duties.

As we will note later (pp. 37-38), the Learned-Sills report of 1922 on Maritime Education commented unfavorably on St. Dunstan's. Whereupon, in an astonishing statement quoted by Professor MacDonald, the Rector, Rev. G.J. McLellan, declared that "it would be better to have young men and women of mediocre attainments intellectually and sterling character than intellectual giants of unreliable character and morals . . . "[10] These careless phrases suggest a reverse snobbery directed against standards. Indeed, the statement was naïve and dangerous, and had no basis in fact. There is nothing sterling about mediocrity, and no evidence that unreliable character and morals are more prevalent among intellectuals than mediocrities. Unfortunately these suggestions were often bandied about by clergy and laymen criticizing Prince of Wales' high standards. So was that grossly unfair word "godless," so often used against public schools and fired at Prince of Wales from time to time. I always replied to this approach by asking for even the slightest indication that St. Dunstan's students and graduates were more religious or moral than those of Prince of Wales. I never got it, and Professor MacDonald's book furnishes no evidence on the subject either.

All this is background for what we will discuss later: Bishop Malcolm MacEachern's statement to his priests in 1966 that "St. Dunstan's must be the foundation on which the structure of higher education and adult education for the future is built." The wonder is that the statement, discussed in Appendix E, was not repudiated immediately by politicians and other Island clergy, because nowhere in Canada outside Quebec, and probably nowhere else in the Commonwealth, would a bishop dare to make the astonishing suggestion that a Catholic seminary should be the model for a country's post secondary public education. And it was incredible that the Island allowed its bishop to get his idea implemented.

But that was not all. Pretentions of a religiously superior community were demolished by church politics, which not only added more reasons why the union of colleges was wrong, but also did enough damage to the Island to hold it back for generations to come.

Clergy and laity raised obstacles to Prince of Wales at every stage of its early development. But the College thrived because, with its Board of Trustees, it had some protection and encouragement during the scandals of those years. Therefore, from the church standpoint, the Board had to go. When troubles went underground during attempts to create some visible harmony, the friends of Prince of Wales in the government retired from the fray for the sake of "peace." But the Catholic activists did not follow, and church and state joined behind the scenes with the powerful combination of Bishop Peter McIntyre and Premier W.W. Sullivan.

They made a daring coup and got away with it. The work and future of Prince of Wales were permanently handicapped when the Board she had since 1834 was abolished when Sullivan took office in 1879. A new board was not to be set up until 1954, by then too late. Thus the public College was left to the mercies of politics and the church.

Without a board of its own Prince of Wales was dependent on a grossly inefficient and politicized provincial board of education, and had no support from Premier Sullivan. St. Dunstan's had its own board, the Bishop and his diocese, and the Catholic Premier as active supporters. In a very short time,

Prince of Wales was helpless in the face of a tragedy that in 1907 killed the Island's greatest opportunity for expanding post-secondary education.

Sir William Macdonald of tobacco fame, an Islander by birth, and an alumnus of Prince of Wales, had maintained an interest in the Island. As a philanthropist he proposed, through McGill University, to finance the expansion to degree-granting status of certain small colleges in Vancouver, Victoria, Guelph, and Montreal as well as Prince of Wales. The proposal made to the various authorities involved a temporary affiliation with McGill, and for awhile the granting of McGill degrees, from which stage full independent university status would follow. For Prince of Wales, in addition to arts and science faculties, an agricultural college was proposed with all appropriate facilities to serve the whole Atlantic region.

Everyone else accepted this generous and splendid plan, and their colleges flourished into fine universities.[11] The Island government, led by a lacklustre Premier, Arthur Peters, approved of the plan too. Both McGill and the government agreed on the details which were to come into effect on July 1, 1907. As for the Island public, the Premier reported "a strong sentiment among many of our people that this affiliation would be a good thing for our Province."[12]

Despite the approval of the plan by Macdonald, McGill, Prince of Wales, the Island government, and the people, church politicians intervened.

The official correspondence tells an astonishing story. The plan was supported with enthusiasm by both McGill and the Island government. "The question has been up for some little time," wrote Premier Peters to the McGill Registrar, "before our Government and Board of Education to get our College – Prince of Wales – affiliated with McGill. We have a very fine College and since the improvements made by Sir William Macdonald, which will be completed this fall, it cannot be equalled in the Maritime Provinces."[13] In reply, Registrar J.A. Nicholson said "I am delighted to learn of your interest in the proposed scheme . . . and am quite satisfied that with your influence and assistance the matter can be consummated."[14] The Premier returned another letter immediately to "assure you that myself and the Government here will do all we can to secure the affiliation. . . . I am very pleased . . . and feel so confident that it can be carried out."[15]

The plan then came up before the McGill Faculty. The Vice Principal and Dean of Arts, Charles E. Moyse, reported to the Premier that "the opinion was freely expressed that some official connection between Prince of Wales College and the University was desirable not only on account of the thorough preparation of the many excellent students who have come to McGill from that College, but also because the expansion and consolidation of our academic interests seems more than ever forced upon us by our national outlook."[16] Three days later Premier Peters wrote to the General Passenger Agent of the Intercolonial Railway asking for a pass for the McGill Registrar who was to visit the Island, and told him that "Prince of Wales College is being very much enlarged by Sir William Macdonald and is likely to be one of the finest colleges in the Maritime Provinces."[17]

"Prince of Wales College being thus made a College of McGill University," the Registrar wrote to the Premier, "the Professors will be professors of a College of McGill University and as such will have a status which they had not before. . . . I trust that nothing will stand in the way of this much-to-be-desired result."[18] A bill was drafted and sent to McGill on March 18, 1907 by the Premier. It was in the Premier's name and it designated Prince of Wales as "The Prince of Wales College of McGill University" providing courses of study leading to degrees at McGill, which arrangement was modelled on that of Vancouver College, later the provincial University of British Columbia. Nicholson then advised Peters that "The question of the institution of Prince of Wales College of Prince Edward Island as a College of McGill University has gone through its final stage in so far as the University is concerned, Corporation having approved of the proposal at a meeting held on the 3rd inst."[19]

The blow then fell.

When acknowledging McGill's approval on April 17, Premier Peters wrote that "I am sorry to have to tell you that for the present year we do not propose to carry out this proposition. . . . The House has received a number of petitions from Farmers' institutes complaining that more money should not be expended on University Education before we have expended some additional on Agricultural Education" . . . the matter was to "stand over for another year." On April 25 the Premier told McGill that the institutes and agricultural community "seem to think that the affiliation will cost the Province a large sum of money," this despite Sir William Macdonald's generosity, and the inclusion of an agricultural college in the plan! Peters did promise to "take measures this season to in some way obtain an expression of opinion from the different centres of education on the Island on this matter."

This wishy-washy tactic was fatal. As the Duff-Berdahl report on education quoted later, "If one consults a sufficiently large number of people for a long enough time, one can develop insurmountable opposition to the most innocuous idea."[20] This was especially true on the Island when Prince of Wales had no board of governors to handle its interests with McGill, and to meet opposition with facts rather than be stampeded by fear. A weak premier will not face a strong church. A strong premier will not just consider the merits of a policy if there is a good board, but will also face down a threatened row or loss of votes. An average premier need only refer critical predators to a college board of governors for fearless answers.

Thus Prince of Wales and the province lost a rare and priceless opportunity that would have enormously enhanced the interests of the Island's people and the Maritime economy from that day to this.

I asked Premier J. Walter Jones for his opinion of this proposal and its result. He was a professional agriculturalist who had contacts with Sir William Macdonald, and had been principal of the Macdonald Consolidated School which had been endowed by the philanthropist. He was a leader in farming circles on the Island. He turned the air blue with his account of mischief behind the scenes. The government had told McGill that farmers were suspicious of the proposal whereas, Mr. Jones said, it was a well-organized Catholic lobby that went among farmers and local groups and frightened the Cabinet and its weak Premier. His comments confirmed what I had heard from McGill professors who had been involved, of whom I knew four. The action featured the "confidential without public discussion" tactic described in later pages (pp. 114-115) and the cowardice of those who knew the proposal was a great opportunity for the province, but did not have the honesty or courage to stand up to church pressure, even to demand open public discussion. It was a great day for St. Dunstan's when Prince of Wales' wings were thus clipped, but a tragedy for everyone else. For Sir William Macdonald it was the end of his interest in the Island. The event was an example of the old truism that Maritimers are experts at "shooting themselves in the foot," for which habit they pay an enormous price, especially when a church pulls the trigger.

For unbelievable politics it is hard to match still another issue which followed a few years after the death of the Macdonald/McGill/Prince of Wales plan. That the perpetrators were permitted to get away with it is a sad reflection on the character of Island Catholic and Protestant clergy and laity who allowed one great mistake to be followed by another.

The event was an episcopal coup as Catholic clergy and politicians rail-roaded through a silent Legislature an act to incorporate St. Dunstan's as a university. The Macdonald offer must have appeared to the Bishop as a threat to his control, although it need not have been if the Bishop himself had got out of St. Dunstan's way. He must have resented the fact that St. Dunstan's was not asked to join the plan; but its standards were not high enough, and its identity was church-bound, not university related. He and his colleagues appeared unable to tolerate Prince of Wales' recognition and progress, and wanted their much less effective idea of a university on the Island, as Bishop McEachern later put it, to be the "foundation for the future."

This was the dog-in-the-manger approach, and the carefully managed government and Protestant clergy figuratively patted the dog. Thus encouraged, Catholic authorities determined to get for St. Dunstan's the university charter they had prevented Prince of Wales from getting – even though they did not have the opportunity for necessary funds like Prince of Wales had from Sir William Macdonald, or the cooperation and colleagueship of an eminent senior university that Prince of Wales had been offered, or any of the staff, faculties, and standards needed for a university. Indeed, it would have been so easy and sensible for any good political leader to say to St. Dunstan's and the Bishop "you block the larger plan and you need never come to our people for funds or privileges in the future. We will tell the people that loud and clear and furnish them with details of the project and copies of the correspondence." In the face of such an unassailable ultimatum it is doubtful if the Bishop would have dared proceed with his plans. But, as with all church politics, it was easy to placate the naïve with "good will" and proceed behind the scenes with contrived silence.

For authenticity, and bearing in mind the episcopal power behind the union issue of later years, it is revealing to cite Professor MacDonald's account of how the new charter for St. Dunstan's was won in 1917. Bishop Henry O'Leary, he wrote, "headed the three-man committee appointed to prepare the bill and make straight its path through the provincial legislature [and] privately asked the Minister Without Portfolio, Hon. A.E. Arsenault, to pilot it through the upcoming session of the House. . . . Arsenault consented, suggesting only that 'it would be well to mention the matter to Mr. Johnson [an influential Catholic opposition member] in order to make sure that there will be no objection taken. By enlisting his sympathy towards the bill it will greatly assist its passage through the House and probably avoid a discussion, which would not be desirable' . . . *overt* religious controversy was to be avoided at all costs. . . . The bill was passed into law on a voice vote on April 20, 1917 with only minor amendments. The Bishop's careful preparations had paid off. With a minimum of fuss, the University had its charter."[21]

"The true value of the new Act," continued Professor MacDonald, "[was that it] opened the door for St. Dunstan's to expand whenever and in whatever direction is desired." "The University charter," wrote Archbishop A.A. Sinnott of Winnipeg to Bishop Henry O'Leary, "will give you a free hand, and in my opinion you are wise in securing it while you can."[22]

The Macdonald/McGill/Prince of Wales issue and the St. Dunstan's incorporation raise important questions about the calibre of the two colleges. The answers were provided at the time with expert authority by the Learned-Sills Report on Education in the Maritime Provinces of Canada which appeared in 1922, and which, I noted earlier, did not please Rector G.J. McLellan.[23] They were later to destroy the credibility of Bishop MacEachern's letter to his priests discussed in Appendix E.

The staff of St. Dunstan's, five years *after* it got university status, said the report, "is composed of eight priests and one layman. . . . The classrooms and recreation rooms are bare of equipment. There is no scientific apparatus of any description for any purpose. There is a small library (5 000 to 6 000 volumes) that appears to be used only by the priests. . . . The college has never given its own degree, tho recently empowered to do so by the legislature, and it does not intend to do so in the immediate future. St. Dunstan's has a magnificent farm on which, in such a community, agricultural courses should long since have been flourishing." But the college had failed to provide this and other services "to stir from its apparent torpor the population of one of the most beautiful spots in the north."[24] With positive change, St. Dunstan's "would naturally throw its lot in with St. Francis Xavier."

On the other hand, continued the report, "Prince of Wales College is doing a careful and thorough work in its secondary field, and its selected students (those taking senior matriculation) are among the best wherever they go. Some of these have led their class at graduation from college, and bear witness to the successful selection of the process thru which they are put."[25]

Three conclusions are unavoidable. It was only church tactics, not academic credentials or financial facts, that prevented the more academically favored Prince of Wales from becoming the Island's preeminent university through the academic arrangements made with McGill, and the financial provisions made by Sir William Macdonald. Only the strongest of condemnatory adjectives are appropriate to describe how eight priests and a layman with a powerful bishop as an active politicized chancellor, were first foisted on the Legislature as a "university," and then permitted to dawdle along without doing the duty entrusted to them. Authorities in both government and St. Dunstan's obviously had no idea of what a university was; after the negotiations with McGill and Sir William Macdonald, Prince of Wales did. Premier Walter Jones also held this view 27 years later when I was appointed principal of Prince of Wales in 1949. St. Dunstan's had done very little with the mandate the Bishop had snatched and, except for officially-required pre-medical biological courses, its standards were low. The Premier indicated in words similar to those of Learned and Sills that it was time for a change, to allow Prince of Wales "to stir the population" of the Island from "its apparent torpor." This the Reverences would not permit.

One is lead to conclude from the events that, in any showdown, the church is more powerful than the Island government and legislature. Church politics masquerading as religion are stronger and more ruthless (or, on the Protestant side, weaker and more timid) than either religion or state politics. And a strong bishop can overwhelm a weak premier with ease. Both "Christian soldiers marching as to war" in state business, and those who will not "dare to be a Daniel" or "dare to stand alone," are pretty damaging to any state and its people.

Thus, for its only university, the Islanders were persuaded to give up the opportunity of getting a great public institution at no cost and with impeccable national recognition, and to keep the church seminary instead! If Cardinal Richelieu and Father Joseph could have looked down, or up, depending on the location of their after-life, they would have been delighted with the success of their politics.

Chapter Four
COMMUNITY OF COMMUNITIES

The Richelieu policies, the revocation of the Edict of Nantes, the expulsion from Canada of the Protestant French, the exodus of the Acadians, the treatment of the Indians, the early church hostility to Prince of Wales College and the abolition of its board of governors, the destruction of the Macdonald/McGill/Prince of Wales plan, and the St. Dunstan's incorporation, together reveal in formidable, consistent detail a basic strategy in church politics that leads directly to the Island's college crisis of the 1960s. Indeed, it indicates many characteristics of the Island and Canada.

The basic strategy is a negative one to be seen wherever church politics dominate. It involves corralling powers – that is gathering them in to collect and enclose them – and blocking initiatives that the church does not want others to take. The strategy favors a particular form of administration commonly called a "community of communities," a phrase often used in Canada but not accurately defined.

The strategy is described in frank terms by a Jesuit scholar in the English Jesuit magazine *This Month*. As reviewed by the London *Times* on August 15, 1977, Father Raymond Helmick's opinions concern church politics in Ireland, but they fit exactly the operation of Richelieu's ideas in Canada and the church's administration in Prince Edward Island. "That the situation of clerically dominated life, by no means an essential of Catholic life, should be so critical a factor in the situation of violence must be of the greatest concern not only to the local but to the universal church. When there is an initiative taken by the lay Catholic community that does not originate from or come under control of the clergy, the reaction is uniformly either to coopt it or to ruin it." As for Protestant action, he continued, "the Catholic side is aware that clerical domination has no real relation to their Christian faith . . . if they cannot [support it they] suppress it; and if they cannot suppress, destroy it." The Protestants may want the Catholic Church to take its share of the blame for the results, "but realizing that it would be counter productive to say so abrasively, they keep such opinions to the level of generalities."

Coopt, ruin, suppress, and destroy, as well as confining the opinions of others to generalities, are authoritarian and costly actions for a Christian church in a democratic society. They invite frustrated negative responses from others. They indicate reasons for tumult and failure when church corralling and blocking spill over into public affairs and other aspects of life. The verbs are well illustrated in Island education as the church brought them to bear on Prince of Wales College.

The church political strategy has powerful effects. It indicates how weak governments actually are when dealing with church matters. Politically strong but religiously weak governments can be formed with church political support behind them. Political leadership of churches can be forced on other authorities when it is disguised as religion. Strong critics will take a buffeting and be labelled as villains, perhaps even as atheists when they are really agnostics. If the church finds itself wrong it will usually say nothing with the knowledge that criticism will likely go away. Those easily frightened and led, those who do not think for themselves, and those looking for political support for their own plans may be persuaded into believing they do the "right thing" when following clerical political direction. Even when religion is not involved, citizens are often discouraged from questioning or asking for reform because "you can't oppose religion, or God." Such action means that a church can promote, perhaps even enforce, the theory that it is above the law, and then proceed, as Father Helmick says, to coopt, ruin, suppress, and destroy.

There are many examples throughout the world of massive and often mistaken church interventions in politics prompted by this basic strategy. Two major ones in Canada involve Quebec and Prince Edward Island.

Church interventions have often destroyed two-way relationships of French-English associations which Cardinal Richelieu turned into Catholic-Non-Catholic associations. Sir John A. Macdonald gave helpful advice. And Gérard Pelletier described the practical results.

Part of Sir John's well-known advice on the subject advises the English-Canadian that he "must make friends with the French." Unfortunately few know the second part of his sentence with an obligation of equal importance – "without sacrificing the status of his own race or language." The *whole* statement is practical advice to both sides in any linguistic or church difficulty. It would help Parliament, the legislatures, and the governments which, in one-way church issues, are unable to say and do what they want. It would present the citizenry with two sides of the issues with which to form public opinion.

Coralling powers and blocking initiatives may be helped by what Rev. T.C. Douglas called the use of "religion as a gimmick for gaining political support." The powers may then be shared with strategic political partners whom a church can manage if it is too aggressive, or be managed by if it is too trusting. A distinguished Quebecer described this situation in his province in Premier Duplessis' day, and gave an appropriate warning. Gérard Pelletier told of "the inevitable collusion between an excessive clericalism and a corrupt regime . . . [in which] the spiritual powers had for a long time exceeded their proper role. By dint of taking over functions that were rightly those of the state . . . the churchmen had expanded their empire well beyond its natural frontiers. Henceforth they would pay the price of this mistake."[1]

In a powerful contribution to the literature of federalism, Mr. Pelletier emphasized, "It is important to remind ourselves that in the name of nationalism and religion, Duplessis inflicted upon us a twenty-year reign of lies, injustice and corruption, the systematic misuse of power, the sway of small minds and the triumph of stupidity . . . this man and his regime held back for a quarter of a century Quebec's entry into the modern world. It would be fatal to forget that he did everything possible to turn our population inwards upon itself and isolate it from the world. . . . It would actually be dangerous not to recognize that some of those notions lived on in our collective subconscious and are resurfacing today . . . René Lévesque is right. It would be wrong for us to forget the evil done by that corrupt regime. On the contrary, we must keep it in mind, for fear of slipping again into the same ruts and the same patterns of lies."[2]

What Mr. Pelletier wrote is not well understood by Canadians who are continuously bombarded by fanciful allegations of French suffering from English injustice. The many contributions of English Quebecers to "Quebec's entry into the modern world," the loss to Quebec of the Protestant French, the switch from language to church politics as basic public policy, the trumpeting of persons addicted to trahison des clercs, and the continuation of Richelieu's ideas reinforced by Duplessis' "systematic misuse of power" – all illustrate how Father Helmick's views and Gérard Pelletier's account apply to Canada's current Quebec separatist issue, and how in public and church life "it would be wrong of us to forget the evil done."

But we did forget, as badly managed church-state politics have created an alleged incompatibility between Quebec and the "rest of Canada." Federalism has not failed Canada, church politics has.

I may invoke Cardinal Richelieu again to indicate what in the structure of Prince Edward Island society permits the strategy of corralling powers and blocking initiatives. He might well suggest that it works because the Island is a community of communities planned and controlled over many decades under the watchful eye of the church, and in accordance with the Emperor Constantine's system of administration mentioned earlier. Thus the Island has an imperial church organization in miniature. Remember, the Cardinal could add, that no consistent long-term planning has come from Province House and its many temporary occupants to compare with strategies from the Bishop's palace. Because of the community of communities approach and the presence of episcopal agents in every unit, the church has virtually a veto power over the conduct of provincial affairs. Successive Bishops of Charlotte-town publicly exercise that veto rarely, and only in large matters like Prince of Wales' progress, so that intervention will not be too obvious too often. Otherwise the way the diocese is organized keeps the veto operating automatically by its mere presence.

Much of the character of Prince Edward Island's public and educational life results from being a community of communities. This phrase, bandied about during Canada's constitutional discussions, has not been widely accepted. It appears to limit the identity and activity of individual citizens, like a cattle farm with animals herded in separate fenced-off fields. And it seems to compete with and reduce people's identification with their country and loyalty to it. The reason is apparent on the Island at least; it is a tiny community of *innumerable* communities. Indeed its experience suggests a basic principle that a community of communities will not work if there are too many communities in it, especially if some are too big for their location.

The Island is a good example of how a collection of fenced-off citizens works. What we see in practice is not so much a community of communities as an organization of organizations, with countless group activities for small numbers of people, much politics, and many officials at both levels. Fence making and mending take a large proportion of the province's total supply of money and citizens' time and allegiance, leaving that much less for the communities' real work, leisure, and loyalties. The Island's stagnant industries, for example, and losses of economic opportunity are results of the very tight rationing of public and individual initiative and funds among the countless small efforts. And the limited significance of the small units is often compensated for by over-inflated status that easily turns communities into factions and their leaders into potentates and cockalorums.

Emphasis on Island communities reduces attention to individuals. It is too easy to identify people in terms of the communities they belong to rather than their own initiatives and achievements. Their individual personalities may therefore change quickly to the stereotyped personality of one group. Their pride in the province or Canada may decline in relation to their local loyalties to groups and their perceived place in them. For example, the number of obvious potentates and chairmen on Prince Edward Island is far greater than in other provinces. Certainly democracy and citizenship do thrive on effective group action, but only in balance. If individuals are organized too much into too many groups at the same time, individualism dies and groups lose much of their character and become overly standardized collectivities. They then become too easily controlled. One can make an interesting estimate of time and effort devoted in just one day among the P.E.I. population to group enterprises like all the service clubs, church women's organizations, lodge meetings, and countless other such gatherings.

The effects of exaggerated group identifications are often seen in an individual's occupational, family, and social life. Excessive group work may become little more than the activities of a social or political club taking so much time and talent that a member plays a diminished role as a spouse, parent, and productive citizen. If he is careless about direct service to his religious obligations and becomes too much a church politician, his church allegiance or activity may tend to furnish escape from reality, alternatives to responsibility, perhaps even a stamp of allegedly moral approval for belligerency or wrong. "Tis too much prov'd," said Polonius, "that with devotion's visage and pious action we do sugar o'er the devil himself."

This phenomenon, often a result of fashion or decree, may force people to hold ideas and opinions and enjoy privileges and rights only through their membership in some group. Indeed democracy itself may ultimately be regarded as freedom for groups within which individual freedom and initiative are strictly subordinate and controlled. Politicians may be pressured into regarding group responsibility as supreme in their communities, rivalling even legislative leadership. During Canada's constitutional discussions of the 1980s it was remarkable to see factional leaders rising like mushrooms and assuming poses of would-be statesmen.

In Prince Edward Island there are very few practising individualists in the small communities, and they are rare in the top levels of public life. The territories are too small and the fences too numerous and high. Political vision is distorted, like the view of a large TV screen in a clothes closet. Not enough attention is paid to the difference between a community composed of individuals with some individualists among them, and one composed of people who are mere units in groups. In church communities it may not be for nothing that a clergyman's congregation is called his "flock," which dictionaries define as a group that is "kept together, like sheep, goats, geese and," says Webster, "members of a church."

Being kept together may involve the tyranny of dogma, to the point where individualism is sacrificed to mere allegiance to one idea, as it is in many authoritarian groups. People can then be persuaded to do things they would never do as individuals, and the more they do it, even if wrong, the more it is made to appear to be "loyalty" and "duty." Group fanaticism often follows, and violence may become a habit. When commenting on international problems on a visit to Canada, Mikhail Gorbachev indicated that "for me, it is very worrisome that people are beginning to get used to wars and bloodshed."[3] Canadians, in turn, are becoming accustomed to group aggrandizement and conflict, and often accept it as a normal routine.

A community of communities may confuse the terms "community" and "faction." Community is a wide term embracing a group of people sharing loyalties, similar interests, or social or professional affiliations. The emphasis is on groups of individuals, neighborhood, sharing, cooperating, and enjoying or doing things in common. On the other hand the Oxford dictionary defines "faction" as a "self-interested, turbulent, or unscrupulous party" which Webster states is "usually in opposition to the principles or aims of the main body or leadership." It also implies a clique or "exclusive circle of people," or a snobbish or narrow coterie. These definitions deserve serious thought by churches because, without safeguards, their members are easily made factional. Church cults are among the most tragic examples of factions, such as those seen in the deadly extremes of Jonestown and Waco.

Governments and political parties feel the excessive group pressure that affects the legislatures. "Increasingly," writes Jeffrey Simpson, "citizens press their claims through interest groups rather than political parties. In a superficial sense, Ottawa has responded to these groups by creating new ministries to deal with them. In a more profound sense, it has felt compelled to buy the groups off with the only weapon it can muster – chunks of money or, failing that, policies that make life more secure for the interest group in question."[4]

This last is the basic problem in a community – when the administration and work of its constituent communities are devoted more to maintaining and increasing their status and powers than to performing the service that was the only reason for their existence.

All this groupism reminds one that the public usually blames governments for their problems, whereas factions cause many of them. Any group hopes to represent and express public opinion, but it rarely assumes responsibility, accepts blame, or apologizes for mistakes. It does its representing especially badly when it develops a psychological disorder that causes a mental slide from race to racism, religion to religiosity, citizenship to dependence and conformity, and sincere belief to an enticing "ism." Then people may become only enthusiasts with no real belief or identity at all. (The *Globe and Mail* presented some advice. "When birds of a feather flock together, don't get underneath them."[5])

Allegiance to groups is often advertised in a community of communities by excessive identification and labelling. Prince Edward Island is noted for this. There, for example, I could not help but know the church affiliation of every acquaintance from fellow pupils in public and separate schools to people I knew in professional, business, and social life. (Appendix C shows that is still recognized by clergy and laity.) By contrast, after 25 years at the University of Calgary, I was working with 33 colleagues in our department of whose church affiliations I knew only nine. I still have no idea what churches my doctor and dentist attend, or if they attend at all. The Calgary situation is by far the happier and healthier one, because people should be respected for fulfilling their own personal religious commitments, not for advertising their church categories to others.

Closely associated with the ideas of a community of communities are separate schools. Their relevance to the Island's college dilemma of 1968 is forceful because the theory of separate schools was basic to St. Dunstan's, and was used by its devotees among the citizenry as a handy emotional weapon against Prince of Wales. Although the publicly-owned College was founded to serve students of all denominations, which it did very well, it suffered from the strategy of destruction described by Father Helmick. The Catholic clergy, and some Protestant ones too, thought the only way to have a religious dimension in an institution was for the church to control that dimension directly, preferably from within. In practice this assumption is not true. Many clergymen are not able to do it properly, especially if they do not understand young people generally, think in terms of proselytizing, meddle in the other dimensions, and reflect the state of mind of groups of bachelors who set standards and direct administration.

We will meet this subject again in later pages (pp. 64-66, 72), but two basic facts should be introduced here. Prince of Wales and its students always had direct relations with all the churches through student programs, and they did it on their own terms and initiatives, not on those of the churches, which accounts for the harmony and cooperation that prevailed. Furthermore, there is not the slightest indication that Prince of Wales staff and students were any less religious or moral than those of church colleges.

Nevertheless, separate school theories were common on the Island. They flowed over into post-secondary education and into employment and community affairs and caused many problems. Consequently, religion and church politics in education invite some observations by clerics and authorities on how the principle of separate schools operates in practice, especially when it opposes the principle of public ownership, and above all when it introduces Father Helmick's verbs – coopt, ruin, suppress, and destroy.

Furthermore, the word "godless" was used so often by clerics and laymen to describe public schools in the always bitter "separate school questions" of Canadian history, and then used by them against Prince of Wales in the college issue, that it seems desirable to examine briefly some assumptions of alleged divine and devilish auspices. (See appendices C and E as indications of why this subject deserves careful attention.)

The world-wide tactic of separate schools sets up a huge system of administering citizens from birth to death. "Give us your children early," runs an old saying, "and we will control them for life." The policy is arguable because Christianity appears to condemn it. "Suffer little children to come unto me. Forbid them not . . ." does not mean "divide little children into two categories and either forbid them and their teachers to proceed together to me and to life in harmony and love, or make it as difficult as possible for them to do it." Because of the many denominations, religion itself is not taught in separate schools – only one church's interpretation of religion. Education does not appear a concern when it is distorted by being strained through a single set of preconceived church ideas and policies.

These limitations together with recent troubles in church schools have raised much discussion. A deep impression was made in Alberta, for example, by the testimony of a respected Jewish M.L.A. shortly before his death. Sheldon Chumir "reluctantly got into politics" when he saw "what single-minded fanaticism, what intolerance and bigotry, what fear of other people, beliefs and values can do to children, who are all our futures. The central issue is what kind of society do we want to live in, in the future? If we segregate school children from each other on the basis of religion, race or wealth, we will ultimately end up with a society divided in this manner. . . . It makes no sense to spend a great deal of time and money on commissions studying tolerance and understanding and then use our tax dollars to segregate children and encourage social divisions."[6]

The Ontario taxpayers were also reminded of their duty to ask financial questions in 1985 and 1992. Society, said a *Globe and Mail* editorial, "is under no obligation to subsidize segregation. Which is just what public funding for religious schools entails. . . . Where then to draw the line in public funding? Where disintegration of the school system crosses over into disintegration of society."[7]

For this discussion we need not make observations. Rather we should note how church authorities themselves explain and illustrate, first, what they mean by their policy of separate schools; second, the extent to which clergy themselves believe in the policy; and third, the results. Above all, church authorities should be looked to for evidence to support claims that their children are more religious, or finer people, or better citizens, or more assured of the blessings of an afterlife, than the children of other faiths.

The policy of separate schools is emphasized at the top of the hierarchy. They have, said the Ontario Conference of Catholic Bishops, "an awesome privilege and responsibility to create a faith community in their midst . . . where young people experience the church as an alternative community which is shaped more by faith . . . than the values of our consumer culture. . . . "[8] A chairman of the Conference, Bishop Thomas Fulton, announced a new Institute for Catholic Education "intended to encourage and bring closer together the efforts of all Catholic school education in promoting and developing a school system animated by the gospel and respecting the tenets of the Catholic faith."[9] Another aim was declared by Bishop James Doyle, chairman of the Ontario Bishop's Education Commission, "to discover how such areas as curriculum development and teacher-education might be further penetrated by our philosophy of Catholic education."[10]

Non-Catholic teachers would not be acceptable, declared Msgr. Dennis Murphy of the Institute for Catholic Education. "The basic reason to have a Catholic school is that the faith and values are transmitted in a community context. If you dilute the level of faith in the school, it has its effect and if you have as many non-Catholics as Catholics (teaching in the separate schools) you would be seriously compromised."[11] The Pope himself has given clear direction. He told the bishops of the Dominican Republic in 1992 "to infuse a dynamic apostolic renovation in every diocese, parish, community, association and movement of the Latin American church."[12] This is a good illustration of a community of communities on a very large scale, and its administrative practice.

These assertions are controversial enough to require questioning. But their obvious corollary is an insulting idea that other people's efforts are "godless." Msgr. Murphy's words are clear for Catholics, but have not members of other faiths an equal right to use them? Could they say that one of the weaknesses of a community of communities is transmitting "faith and values" in a "community context?" If separate schools could be "seriously compromised" with non-Catholics teaching Catholics, could other Christians say the same thing about Catholics teaching in a public system? What evidence is there that the "level of faith" is "diluted" in a public system? May it not be strengthened by associations with other faiths?

These questions are so important that they supersede Catholic reliance on constitutional guarantees for separate schools in Canada which has been developed into, and carried on as, an exclusive monopoly right not available to others of different denominations. If suggestions for abolishing these guarantees raise objections, the obvious precedent is the far more serious abolition by Catholic authorities of the personal and religious rights of the French-Canadian Protestants, that was described in chapter 2.

The second question to the clergy – on the extent to which they themselves believe in the virtues of separate schools – has been answered by the actions of some priests. Our contemporary society learned with shock about child abuse in Catholic schools by priests and brothers throughout Canada and the United States. The National Catholic Reporter described "a pattern of institutional coverup" in which "known offenders, rather than being removed from the ministry, had been quietly transferred to new posts and, in some documented cases, continued to molest dozens of children for years."[13]

"It's cynical," said Jason Berry, a writer for the Reporter, "it's a complete betrayal of the church's position on the sanctity of life."[14] And Thomas Doyle, a former Vatican diplomat who investigated cases for the Vatican, thought pedophilia "the most serious problem the church has faced in centuries."[15] In their own defence, priests may cite pedophilia in other groups; but others do not also insist on their own moral authority in such matters. In any event, pedophilia is a serious problem for those advocating separate schools.

The question is no longer hypothetical in Canada; the evidence is too strong. In native institutions alone, reported Phil Fontaine, leader of the Assembly of Manitoba Chiefs, many children had been "physically and sexually abused at 60 church-run schools . . . many of them are now in penal institutions. A lot of what they learned in residential schools, they inflict on others."[16] In Quebec four thousand children were reported abused with more expected as people came forward.[17] In Newfoundland the evidence is overwhelming. Michael Valpy reported that the relationship "between many of the people . . . and their clergy was medieval." The power of priests "in the small communities . . . was an unhealthy power. . . . One of the many mysteries about Mount Cashel is how such a place could have been allowed to exist in mid-1970s Canada."[18]

A Canadian historian indicated that it would not be a reform just to replace clerics with laymen. "We must have schools," said Laurier LaPierre, "that can't be dictated to by popes, bishops or priests. Why should any religious denomination illuminate knowledge?" Professor John Snyder of King's College, University of Western Ontario, evidently went further: "Perhaps the real problem is not with denominational schools but with Catholicism. . . . It is becoming 'increasingly embarrassing' for Catholics to defend such doctrines as papal infallibility and birth control, and to continue to support what some believe is a 'closed-mind theology.'"[19]

Our third question for clergy on separate schools concerns results. We have noted the separation and abuse of small children. Another result is well described by an eminent educational authority in South Africa. "You either have to teach children to know and love each other at school benches or they will get to know each other in trenches and on the street corners of burning townships."[20] These words, now tragically illustrated in so many parts of the world and on television, apply to Ireland too, a charming country of charming people, whose chief enemies are those in their midst who play church politics to the death with the two Irelands, often financed by co-religionists in other countries, particularly the United States. An Irish ambulance attendent accustomed to gathering up "people gunned down, blown up, caught in crossfires or just cruelly beaten," had little hope for a real peace, "There's too much history, too many priests, and too many politicians."[21] *Macleans* displayed a title page announcing "God's New Militants, From Ireland to Iran, Religious Warfare is Inflaming the State."[22] The militants are numerous, but evidence that they are God's is non-existent. In the article, Irish Senator Donal Lydon testified that, "The Church has contacts at every level of society, in every corner. Its influence is everywhere. Any politician who ignores the views of the church would have to be crazy." A high proportion of these contacts are first made in separate schools and they are used to organize opinion and action in community affairs, especially in communities of communities. This is probably the real purpose of separate schools everywhere and the chief reason for criticizing them as political units in church politics.

Two lively Canadian issues describe the church politics of educational separatism, the Prince Edward Island college issue, and the Ontario separate schools question of the late 1980s. The rest of this book will be devoted to the Island problem in its local and national aspects. Since it slipped through public opinion with so much secrecy that Islanders never knew the implications of it, we may profitably examine briefly the Ontario event to throw extra light on the subject.

The Ontario separate schools debate has been controversial and costly for many years, as well as bad advertising for Christian unity. There is nothing ecumenical about separate schools. Practically every principle of democracy in legislative and cabinet government was violated in the interest of Ontario separate schools in 1985. The strategy seemed designed to please the Cardinal Archbishop of Toronto, embarrass the Anglican Archbishop of Toronto, stampede the Premier of Ontario and his colleagues, and give waverers every excuse to sit back and do nothing.

An authoritative description of what happened is in Clair Hoy's biography of Premier William Davis. The Premier, on his own, reports the author, had promised the Cardinal privately that "he would end the 100 year old dispute by extending public aid to Roman Catholic Separate Schools beyond Grade 10, to Grades 11, 12 and 13. Apparently Davis had not told his advisors or the Cabinet. Everybody was absolutely stunned."[23]

At his colleagues' demand Davis called on the Cardinal and explained that the time was not ripe for such a move just before a possible election and a visit by the Pope. "But this time," writes the biographer, "the cardinal, whom the opposition consistently accused of being too cosy with Davis, with considerable justification, wasn't buying. He told Davis he was shocked he'd try to renege on a deal. He said he was a man of his word, a man of honor, and he couldn't believe he would back out. And the cardinal hit him with the big stick and said 'if you want to run an election without keeping your word count on having opposition from every pulpit in every Catholic church in Ontario.' Well, Davis just folded like a three-dollar accordion. That's why there was no election. Nobody will talk about it, but that is what happened."[24]

After the necessary legislation was passed, R.A. Dodds, Director of Education of East York, discussed the shuffling around of students and public schools to suit the separate schools. He reported the chairman of the Toronto board as saying that "we are witnessing a land grab unparalleled in this province, and it is only the beginning." He himself said that "hundreds of millions of dollars have been spent to create a separate secondary school system and not one of those dollars was spent to improve the quality of education or to reduce the dropout rate."[25]

An even more fundamental problem in this crisis was the lack of the democratic right to discuss and disagree. The Catholics had literally a free and private hand and their Cardinal was in full control. Whereupon Anglican Archbishop Lewis Garnsworthy made an understandable public statement on the tactics used: "This is the way Hitler changed education in Germany." The statement was true and the fact well known. But Archbishop Garnsworthy was heavily criticized for using the comparison with Hitler. Premier Frank Miller, campaigning in an election after succeeding Davis, declared that "Garnsworthy's intemperate comments could rekindle the kind of religious prejudice that had been an unfortunate part of Ontario's history."[26] This sent the timid scurrying for cover. The Premier did not dare to say the same thing about the Cardinal who had already rekindled the prejudice. Nor would he ask who kept the issue going for a century, and whether the reasons for doing it were valid.

This, with variations, is what happened in the Island's college issue, with me in the unfortunate position of Archbishop Garnsworthy.

Any discussion of church politics in a community of communities always indicates how people fear to think and speak out, thus permitting other people to think for them and control them. It seems irreligious for religion to be considered the most bitterly divisive subject for fearful discussion in every part of the world.

Frankness on this subject could be expected from H.L. Mencken, the acerbic observer of human nature. "The deepest and most widespread of human weaknesses is intellectual cowardice, the craven appetite for mental ease and security, the fear of thinking things out." This comment is a reminder of what has been called "feel-good theology." For some who talk of liberty the "pious exercises may be no more than an effort to get into Heaven by false pretenses."[27] John Buchan (Lord Tweedsmuir) commented on how unreliable such people are. "Saints were no doubt sure of their portion in the next world, but they were often a feeble and uncomfortable folk in the present one."[28]

An important observation came from the distinguished political scientist Walter Bagehot. He described a situation where "tolerance too is learned in discussion, and, as history shows, is only so learned. In all customary societies bigotry is the ruling principle . . . any one who says anything new is looked on with suspicion, and is persecuted by opinion if not injured in penalty. One of the greatest pains of human nature is the pain of a new idea. It is, as common people say, so 'upsetting,' it makes you think that, after all, your favorite notion may be wrong, your firmest beliefs ill-founded. . . . Naturally, therefore, common men hate a new idea, and are disposed more or less to ill-treat the original man who brings it. . . . But discussion, to be successful, requires tolerance. It fails wherever, as in a French political assembly, any one who hears anything which he dislikes tries to howl it down."[29]

Former Prime Minister Pierre Trudeau had an insight into this subject. He told Conrad Black that French Canadians "like a winner and mercilessly boo a loser, and English Canadians indulge a loser and, for reasons I have never understood, lustily boo a winner." Mr. Black himself indicates that the one "laid low" may be "the one whose destruction would most frighten the others."[30]

These views recall parliamentary traditions with responsible government, oppositions, and legislative privileges, and educational traditions which feature freedom of thought to expand the capacity and judgment of the mind. Unfortunately many clerics violate these traditions, the autocratic ones by silencing opposition to get their way, and the weak ones by living off the avails of autocracy. As for new ideas, a young man explained in 1988 what it is like growing up in Prince Edward Island, "It's a good place to live, as long as you don't try to be too different. It's getting better. A couple of years ago if you wore a pink shirt you were dead."[31] This slow pace of change is caused by an almost total lack of real and frank two-way discussion about controversy among the fenced-off citizens in controlled Island communities, especially in those where church politics are dominant. Many will shake their heads, but few will commit themselves.

The tactic of discouraging thought, discussion, and criticism is reinforced in autocratic churches by a powerful strategy of debasement, the impact of which is enormous in the units of a community of communities. The Vatican's Joseph Cardinal Ratzinger was specific when visiting Toronto. "The church's main job is the care of the faith of the simple. A truly reverential awe should arise from this which becomes an internal rule of thumb for every theologian."[32] Faith of the simple? truly reverential awe? in a democracy?

All these problems may bedevil any community of communities. Now let us watch them do it in Prince Edward Island, where churches illustrate political power, both in a small place and on a national scale.

Chapter Five
TO PRINCE OF WALES COLLEGE

I was asked in 1949 to go to Prince of Wales College as its principal. I had once been a student there and loved it, but I had had no contact with it since. I was content with teaching political science at Carleton in Ottawa, and enjoyed life in the Capital. I did not know that the then principal was retiring, and I had not made any attempt to get the job, or indeed to move to the Island in any capacity.

It was Premier J. Walter Jones who extended the invitation. He was to be in Oakville, Ontario for a cattle auction, and asked me to join him there as his guest. For a day and a half I wandered around the barns and arenas meeting cattlemen, watching the bidding, and listening to Mr. Jones explain what was going on – and all the while wondering why I was there. Eventually he got to the subject and extended his surprising invitation. "As a cattleman, would he pay you by weight?" asked a friend. He extolled the College and what it meant to the Island. He was well aware of its background and its problems, and he put the proposal as a challenge to do something special for the Island. He also mentioned that Prince of Wales' public relations had slipped and said that some antagonistic churchmen and one or two politicized faculty members were to blame.

It seemed to me there was a challenging job worth doing. I went to the Island to look things over. The Cabinet interviewed me and I spent two days with staff at the College. Carleton said "don't leave" and offered a promotion, and Prince of Wales and the government said "come." My age, 30, was in the Prince of Wales tradition; my best-known predecessors, Principals Anderson and Robertson, were the same age when appointed to the same job. It was the Island, the College, and the Premier that prompted me to accept. I went, and nineteen happy and adventurous years followed. Looking back I would not have missed the experience, because life there was at its very best and very worst. One of my University of Calgary colleagues asked me years later "How could you stand a quiet life in that little province?" I told him one could live there productively and dangerously; and I did.

Three special challenges in the Maritime Provinces were evident in 1949, but few local authorities and citizens would admit the extent of them. All were important to the Island and Prince of Wales.

One of these challenges was a decline in the traditional Maritime reputation for education. Inadequate funds were only part of it. Technical developments during and after the war required many changes in the work of the fourteen universities and colleges in the region. Of these only two, Dalhousie and the University of New Brunswick, were real universities; the rest were colleges. But few people admitted the difference.

As a second challenge, the economy was in doubtful shape. The Royal Commission on Economic Prospects (the Dawson Commission) and the Atlantic Provinces Economic Council suggested many changes, including the development of facilities for research in the universities, colleges, and governments, and the hiring of people who could do it. Another seaside province, Newfoundland, had just been added to the region, and her economy was in a bad way.

The third challenge was in culture. Canada was behind many nations in most cultural activities, and to study them Parliament had just appointed the Royal Commission on the Arts, Letters, and Sciences (the Massey Commission). How far behind the Maritimes were was indicated by two leading citizens. "Nova Scotia," wrote Thomas H. Raddall, the eminent novelist, "was in a cultural ice age, and the pace was glacial."[1] "I can't see," said Premier Jones in 1950 at a government dinner for the Massey Commission, "why the Commission should bother with Prince Edward Island at all; it doesn't need any culture."[2]

These challenges were among the reasons I was attracted to the new job. Premier Jones said that no one on the Island had devoted any interest to what they were actually doing in education and economics. There was, for example, no one in Prince of Wales or St. Dunstan's who, he said, the government could call upon for advice or research. No scholarly work had been done in either place and its value in teaching was not appreciated, a problem shared by several other Maritime institutions. Mr. Jones was not interested in culture at the time, although he had written a useful book on the fur industry, but I suggested that other community activities could not go very far without it.

It was my hope that Prince of Wales would help meet these challenges, and in doing so enhance its own academic teaching facilities and the economic and cultural life of the province. I was well placed to promote this aim soon after I got to the Island. The Social Science Research Council of Canada appointed me to do a survey of research facilities of all the Atlantic universities and colleges. This project provided an opportunity for visits to these institutions which would be of great value in my work.

The Massey Commission visited the Island shortly after I arrived, and I presented to it, and the Island people, the first proposal that led to the Confederation Centre of the Arts. As for economics, the Jones government, and later the A.W. Matheson government, asked me to write briefs for them. They sent me as an Island representative to the Atlantic Provinces Economic Council of which I became president a few years later. Meanwhile I published a book on the Island's political history and government, and taught a full schedule in political science and Canadian history, neither of which, shame to say, had been on the curriculum. The public reaction was a continuing demand for speeches and lectures throughout the Island that provided opportunity to meet its citizens.

At this time and for many years thereafter I was asked the two questions posed to most native Islanders returning or leaving. They illustrate very well what life on the Island is like and how it can affect people and institutions, especially those in schools and colleges.

"Why did you return?" My answer was sincere and I passed it on to prospective new staff members for the College. Physically the province was beautiful, and all its assets were a stone's throw from anyone's home. One could go trout fishing for an hour or two almost any time and get a good catch, and the beaches were nearby, which facilities were often remote and expensive elsewhere. "Outdoors" had an entirely different meaning from that of children growing up in Montreal or Toronto. It was easy to make friends and acquaintances in the small society, and activities were numerous. Many things happened in public affairs because of provincial status; problems and potentates were coming and going. One's hunting instincts could be directed towards sources of funds and outside help. And most important of all was the scope among Islanders for individual initiative in getting, doing, and improving things for themselves, of which few of them had an appreciation.

The answers to "Why do you not go back?" or "Why did you leave?" are often given by non-resident Islanders. They admit the advantages, but condemn their misuse. The convenient enjoyments are so delightful that too many people over-do them and neglect real work; a Coney Island atmosphere hovers over the unwary. The politics and government are overwhelming and Lilliputian, and their productivity is minimal compared with the sound they make and the money they cost. The Island does little for itself and depends too much on Ottawa. The churches are politicized and divisive; gossip is rampant in so small a place; and people who cherish isolation often have narrow outlooks on life.

The year I arrived, to which these comments refer, was 1949. The situation has not seemed to change even four decades later. The president of a major Island business was frank in 1991. "On P.E.I.," Garth Jenkins told a trade seminar, "we have such an easy free ride that we don't really live in the real world. . . . The environment here has been that government sponsors everything. I was shocked [to find out that] 70 per cent of the funds coming into P.E.I. came from government, and 80 per cent of businesses are tied to government. We have it very soft on P.E.I."[3] Surely, said some, the Island needs more to identify itself than Lucy Maud Montgomery. But a *Guardian* editorial on Anne of Green Gables was quoted on attracting tourists: "It's best to flaunt what you've got. And . . . we haven't got much more than Anne."[4] Those who use pride in "the Island way of life" as a reason for lack of development were told by John Morrison of the Canadian Manufacturers' Association that if this "means remaining dependent on Ottawa and being unable to develop its own industrial base . . . that's not a very proud way to live." Nevertheless, replied David Weale, a local opponent of the "fixed link" with the mainland, "modern society is a powerful solvent dissolving traditional culture everywhere . . . . The establishment of a fixed link represents a giant step toward unchecked modernism."[5] But a prominent Island businessman and supporter of the fixed link, Alan Holman, made the basic analysis of the subject: "I think [the fixed link] a wonderful opportunity for the people of the Island to join the rest of the world and earn its own way."[6]

The Government of Prince Edward Island itself described the challenge and sounded the clarion call for change in the Speech from the Throne to the Legislature in 1981, a call which went largely unheeded. "Many of the unrealistic assumptions and expectations of the past few decades must be discarded. A new view of society and of ourselves is required. We must become more self-reliant . . . make more efficient use of resources . . . tailor our expectations to the actual productivity of our economy . . . recognize that our well-being depends on our own initiative and resourcefulness, rather than on the largesse of governments. . . . The future well-being of our province is not a right which can be guaranteed; rather it is a challenging task for which all Islanders must be willing to bear their share of responsibility."[7]

No serious and frank study of this general problem has yet been made. Higher education is part of it and so is church politics. What role did Prince of Wales have in "the Island way of life?"

Prince of Wales was a first class junior college with the final two years of high school, the first two of university, and the normal school for training teachers. It had an excellent reputation for high standards, and its graduates had ready access to employment and the universities. There was good reason for this reputation. The junior college system in North America, along with parallel institutions in Europe, combined the best features of late high school and early university. At Prince of Wales, for example, the two high school years had far more facilities and much better trained teachers than grades 11 and 12 in local high schools. While some students with low marks in provincial examinations thought the transition to the College was demanding, the great majority found the curriculum, facilities, and student activities to be stimulating and enjoyable. Because fire had destroyed the College a few years before, the huge new building was modern and well-equipped. In science, for example, the laboratories were of exceptional quality for high school students because they were also used by the freshman and sophomore years. Those who left at the end of the high school years therefore had a sound preparation for employment or further education.

As for the university years, it was a remarkable feature of junior colleges, which Prince of Wales shared, that so many freshmen students had already had two years in the College. They knew the ropes. The transition to facilities and teachers in a university environment was therefore eased, and the advanced courses were based on a solid foundation. This arrangement operated at a time when high school training was controversial all over America, and numerous experts and commissions, including the Deweyites, were trying to find workable solutions in the post-war world. For example, how should universities serve students in their freshman science classes that came from both high schools that gave good training in science and high schools where science was weak? Too often standards were lowered, or "popular" science was introduced to accommodate both groups. When I went on the staff it was refreshing to note that while this problem was being furiously debated in Ontario, it had long been solved at Prince of Wales and the transitions from year to year were working smoothly.

The training of teachers was also controversial all over the continent – particularly the mixture of "subject courses" and "education courses" in the licencing requirements. Prince of Wales had long had a practical arrangement by which teacher trainees were given the program of academic courses in regular classes with other students, together with courses in "education" and practice teaching. This arrangement resulted in well-rounded students with a combination of subjects and how to teach them.[8]

The last transition for the students was from the sophomore year, the fourth year at Prince of Wales, into the third years of the universities. This had long since been discussed and planned with the universities themselves, especially during the Sir William Macdonald/McGill/Prince of Wales negotiations of 1906-07. Close contacts were maintained with all the universities to which

Prince of Wales students went. But for the maintenance of standards the College enjoyed special relationships with Dalhousie and McGill. If they were happy with our graduates the rest had nothing to complain about.

It was most important to make and keep these arrangements about standards and transitions. This was a major problem in the Maritime Provinces where several of the 14 "universities" developed by adding more of the same to what were essentially high school years. It was sad to watch students in several places spinning their academic wheels in elementary work, and to note unqualified people teaching beyond their depths, sometimes using the title "professor" without justification. Almost as bad was hiring retired people without adequate experience with students. Generally these knew only the small part of a field in which their job had been and had little experience with the rest of it.

Another aspect of standards worked very well. Prince of Wales, which had an excellent program of extra-curricular activities, insisted on one cardinal rule. These activities had to be accompanied by good marks. The value of this rule was appreciated by most students because they honored it and had a greatly enriched college experience. Unfortunately it was not so well recognized in recent years throughout the continent, and too many stars of school and college extra-curricular activities had nowhere to go when their marks and social or athletic skills were not good enough for advanced competition. And, paradoxically, the extra-curricular activities had everywhere diminished in amount and quality among the general rank and file of students, even before the recession began.

I knew the 14 Atlantic universities pretty well after 1949 and sat on boards and committees with their professors and officials. It was my view that the degrees of at least six of the fourteen were then worth less than the graduation certificate of Prince of Wales, despite the two-year difference in time spent. Many authorities agreed with this opinion at the time, although a few thought four a fairer figure. The four were obvious: St. Anne's, St. Thomas, St. Joseph's, and St. Dunstan's. Two others, St. Mary's and Mount St. Vincent, were better than these four because of their surroundings in Halifax which had five universities. Another, King's, had a thin program by itself, but it shared some facilities at Dalhousie. Mt. Allison was then in poor shape and it was reputed across Canada as the place where students rejected elsewhere could be sure to get in. Indeed the Dawson Commission on economic prospects had recommended that Mt. Allison be closed and its campus used as a regional training school for teachers. It improved greatly soon after.

As for my view of these institutions, it was based on standards of admission; the training and abilities of professors as university-level teachers; the number of courses in the upper years that were really upper-level courses and not just more freshman and sophomore-level ones; the time and energy spent by students on academic subjects vital to their training and employment rather than on the "Mickey Mouse" courses; the standing and quality of extra-curricular activities; and the amount of time and remedial work the graduates had to devote elsewhere to bring inadequate qualifications up to standard for jobs and further training. On all these counts, and except for Dalhousie and the University of New Brunswick, Maritime universities were weak at the time in several, or many faculties and departments.

Nevertheless, every one of these institutions was allowed to develop and resisted any idea of union among them. The Catholics kept their eight out of the fourteen, including the six seminaries. The Anglicans sustained Kings College in Halifax. The United Church rallied around Mount Allison in Sackville, N.B. By contrast, with all its assets, Prince of Wales was stopped in its tracks because the Catholic diocese of Charlottetown obstructed it at every turn and Protestant clergy and politicians were too frightened to help in the crisis.

The reason for this unique situation was the College's greatest weakness as a publicly-owned institution. It lacked a suitable non-political board of governors with authority and backed by the sponsorship of the state. Consequently it had no protection against clerical predators. The Island government, conditioned to retreat from controversy, would not defend it. Every college and university in Canada, including all in the Maritimes except Prince of Wales, had its own board of interested governors. The Catholic bishops of Charlottetown took full advantage of this weakness over the years. After Premier Sullivan abolished the Prince of Wales board in 1879 the politicians and faculty got too accustomed to the situation and did nothing about it.

We did make progress. One of the conditions under which I went to Prince of Wales was that there would be no more interference in college policy and business by the Department of Education which, subject to political pressure, had previously been tempted to meddle when it had nothing else to do. That was accepted. Premiers Jones and Matheson were delighted to separate College business from the Department, but they and their immediate successors were reluctant to keep cabinet ministers off the board we got in 1954. When a new board was constituted after the Prince of Wales College Act of 1964, a more normal arrangement began. But the government still appointed the members, and the result was many identities based on church affiliations rather than the interests of the College. There was always one episcopal lay potentate who made his weight felt; cabinet Catholics maintained an unhealthy interest in the appointment of non-Catholic board members too, and favored "nice guys" who were "safe."

The composition of the faculty before 1949 was also influenced by politics and localism. Too high a proportion, indeed almost all of them, were Islanders. I was able to remedy this unhealthy situation with the support of Premiers Jones and Matheson and faculty too. There was a great flutter in the cabinet, legislature, and churches the day we recommended the appointment of one Islander and three non-Islanders! A disturbance came when a "foreigner" with a Ph.D. in French language and literature was appointed instead of a local Acadian B.A. with no experience in either as a subject. The difference, I was told by a cabinet minister, was that an untrained francophone was better for the job than even the best-trained bilingual anglophone! Some complainers were prepared to agree on another Maritimer or two, and we did appoint some. But in doing so we avoided a tendency of Nova Scotian and New Brunswick churches, governments, and universities to dump their unwanted on the Island. This was not a difficult thing to do as local authorities were too fond of taking those who would "come for less."

Prince of Wales had opportunities in the 1950s of tapping Canada's developing cultural resources, and encouraging some of its own. This was "new," so our critics, especially the church ones, did their best to stop such "nonsense." We set up a concert series especially to bring in young newly-trained artists who needed concert opportunities; this we did with the cooperation of the Toronto Conservatory of Music which was developing the plan. We had a close relationship with the Canadian Opera Company and its founder-director Herman Geiger-Torel who came regularly for many years, and was one of the first recipients of our honorary L.L.D. We also went pretty far for our local critics when we produced Gilbert and Sullivan's *Mikado* which had long been a favorite project of colleges and schools from coast to coast. The public, which had not seen an opera produced in Charlottetown since 1912, responded with enthusiasm and packed our large auditorium to overflowing. A church politician and cabinet minister then wanted the government to collect all the money we made on *Mikado* and put it in the consolidated revenue fund of the province. Even the government laughed at that. The Supreme Court greatly enjoyed the comic opera *Trial By Jury* as our guests, but they found even funnier the snorting displeasure of their Chief Justice who lamented the daring parody on Her Majesty's judiciary.

A reader may ask whether it was really true that it was churchmen who led assaults on College projects. The answer was "Yes" in almost every case. The congregations took no action, and most church people were unaware of the sniping done in their name until it had gone too far. But there were clerics and elders afflicted with a kind of political St. Vitus Dance that popped up at the appearance of anything new or controversial during a spell of church politics. Often their participation was of the "feel-good" kind, and they gave little or no thought to whether they had enough knowledge or experience to participate sensibly and effectively.

Other needed cultural activities were started in those years. We invited local groups to produce events in our auditorium on their own initiative. Charlottetown, like most cities, had, for many years, the welcome Community Concerts and Little Theatre and Dominion Drama Festival presentations. They were travelling national and United States enterprises that had been presented locally. Now we were hoping the Islanders would develop new things on their own. Fortunately national, local, and individual cultural enterprises were to combine in the Confederation Centre of the Arts, two blocks from the Prince of Wales campus.

All this academic and cultural service is what the Learned and Sills Report[9] thought the Island needed from education, "to stir from its apparent torpor the population" which had, said the local businessman cited earlier, "such an easy free ride that we don't really live in the real world."

Chapter Six

CHURCH POLITICS

The impact of church politics on Prince of Wales increased dramatically with the province's neglect of modern public administration. Governments elsewhere developed public trusts to handle the many new powers that appeared in the 1930s and 1940s. These trusts combined public responsibility, business and professional practice, and freedom from political interference. They were managed by public boards of directors instead of the civil service, and they ran railways, power companies, communications facilities, regulatory tribunals, and the like, as well as provincially owned post-secondary institutions. Prince Edward Island's government ignored this change and hung on to its old inadequate system of direct political and bureaucratic control. An administrative vacuum appeared because local ministers and civil servants could not handle the new powers and depended on a reluctant Ottawa to tell them what to do and pay their bills. As we shall see in later pages, the government's mistakes resulted in the loss of a Georgetown industrial initiative, a provincial development plan, and Prince of Wales College – all in about six years and at enormous cost.

Something had to rush in and fill the vacuum, and the interloper was church politics. It got in, as it often does, disguised as religion to make people think something right and wonderful was happening and to warn off questioners and opposition.

To appreciate the Island situation we should note some relevant aspects of church politics in general for which the Island provides many examples. Why, it may be asked, should church politics be absent in a public trust? When a legislature assigns powers to a board, it gives the board the responsibility for running a specific enterprise, dealing directly with its personnel and the public, and reporting back annually to the legislature. The board has a direct interest; the enterprise has its own executive that is responsible for management; and, while the state owns the trust, it knows that back-seat driving is dangerous and in normal business lets the board do its job without interference.

Once churches get involved with public enterprise the danger of failure rises. They quarrel among themselves. They like their own independence and insist on "freedom of religion," which is too often freedom for political interference. By and large church personnel have only limited personal experience and knowledge of public affairs. But they may resent other people who wish freedom from church politics. And their tendency to frustrate initiative is an obstacle to enterprise and change.

If a church nominates someone to a sensitive activity he is likely to be an agent for the church rather than a member of the enterprise, voting according to back-stage instructions instead of the demands of the business at hand. Church politicians often seek places on boards from reluctant politicians as rewards for clerics and laymen, or as a means of getting their weak members out of the way. This problem has long been encountered in the chaplaincy service, for example. Churches should never be permitted to nominate chaplains. Hospitals and universities should select their own chaplains on the advice of their own trusted consultants. Churchmen will often pass over ability in favor of political recognition of church status and members. Indeed, all a nominee's commitments will be misdirected if his affiliation and status are the reasons he was appointed.

But is it not democratic for a group to have "representation" on a board? Perhaps, but on a "need to have it" basis, and only if the emphasis is on the job to be done rather than the patronage available. Members of an interest group who are appointed because of their personal qualifications will do more for the board and be better symbols of their affiliation.

And what about concern for church interests in education like holding services, arranging curriculums, providing advice, and teaching theology students? In practice, having clergy or laymen on a board or committee, and giving a special entrée to a denomination, do not automatically benefit religion. Management of religious functions are handled better by a university or college itself through its administration, teaching staff, and advisors, as others of its functions are handled, with clergy used only as consultants as the trust so wishes. The evidence? The well-known weaknesses and low standards of theological studies, the widespread shortage of clergymen, low attendance at church services, the unique bitterness of church relations throughout the world, and the widespread refusal of churches to take responsibility for their mistakes all indicate that clergymen's time and energies are too much devoted to church status and politics and too little devoted to religion.

An experienced appraisal of this subject was given by a Canadian newspaperman who was head of a commission during constitutional discussions, and the chairman of the Radio-Television and Telecommunications Commission. Keith Spicer, when editor of the *Ottawa Citizen,* is quoted as saying "In this country the meddling of turbulent priests in politics has grown so pervasive that it would be frightening if most clerics were not so laughable. . . . The smugness of these ecclesiastical busybodies carries them serenely through any and every political and economic issue. But their know-it-all pride blinds them to the very reasons for their calling: to help the little, ordinary people find God."[1]

This forceful opinion, which is widely shared, prompts detailed discussion about clergy in church politics and of the practical difficulties they encounter. In church politics, that is. I have often heard that very few priests and ministers devoted to church politics are able servants of religion. I suspect that is true, but it is outside the scope of this book. Nevertheless I do know, as do most people and Mr. Spicer himself, that there are exceptions to his comment – clerics of personal and professional distinction who give impeccable service to church and society. Unfortunately they tend to be nudged into the background by the fashionable who have taken too many courses in sociology, who do not know the difference between serving and meddling, and who prefer gossip on the afternoon tea and luncheon circuits when they are not adequately trained or experienced in religion.

Much responsibility for what Mr. Spicer describes lies with the theological colleges. The training of clergy is, with exceptions, woefully weak. Anybody can enter the theology courses which are among the easiest in the universities; virtually everybody passes; the so-called graduate work is usually elementary and unprofessional. A few seek and get strong training and serve with distinction, but it is embarrassing how many students enter theology because they had not succeeded elsewhere and had nowhere else to go, or because their parents steered them towards it.

Churches are responsible for the location of many weak clergy by not selecting carefully. And clerics themselves are not always straightforward in their advice to selection committees. This is a special problem on the Island. Too many inadequate clergy get translated to the province. In episcopal churches bishops often send them to the Island when they cannot find places for them. This practice is obvious; I was told about it in detail by an eminent bishop; and I have known the university reputations of some of the clerics concerned. In churches where ministers are "called," local selection committees may take advice from those who want to dispose of the unsuccessful or find places for the "nice guys." The provincial government has the same problem, and has become well known for it. The Island's military, Mounted Police, and banks, as well as local branches of the federal government, have encountered the problem, but are much better at handling it than the churches and the local government.

Some may believe that clerical influences are surely over, that laymen no longer pay attention to church leaders – in Quebec for example. But they do pay attention on the Catholic side.

Laymen, reported a Rome dispatch, are open to "the accusation that they form a network pursuing a hidden agenda in the church, business and politics."[2] "God," declared Canada's Cardinal Carter, is "assuredly telling us that a new era is at hand and the faithful people, the sacred consecrated Christian laity, must come to the rescue."[3] A well-known authority wrote that after Pope John XXIII's death,"strides were made by Opus Dei in increasing its ultra conservative influence."[4] "They are fanatics," wrote Pauline author Giancarlo Rocca. "For Opus conciliation is defeat. It does not believe in compromise." And, wrote one quoted as leaving Opus after ten years as a member, "Opus has taken over the role traditionally played by the Jesuits in education."[5]

How does this action work in practice? A good example was seen in Ottawa. Prime Minister Trudeau and External Affairs Minister Allan MacEachen were reported to have by-passed the Cabinet, the diplomatic corps, and the public to set up the Vatican representative as an ex-officio dean of the diplomatic corps, at the reputed request of the Archbishop of Ottawa. This practice is often followed in Catholic countries. Criticism caused the next government to revoke the decision.[6] Former Justice Minister E. Davie Fulton was fairly explicit and exclusive on the subject, although he provided no evidence. He is reported to have told a meeting of church laymen in Charlottetown that "the Catholic layman has great obligations to be involved in politics because he is better instructed to bring a Christian and moral judgment on issues that arise [by] official pronouncements of the Church Herself [sic]. This is as I see my role as a Catholic layman, it is not for me to seek the Catholic solution but the prudent, resting assured that the prudent solution will always be the Catholic solution."[7]

"The rules of today's lay people," wrote Jean Guy Dubuc in an editorial of *La Tribune*, Sherbrooke, on August 3, 1991, "are as absolute as for those of yesterday's church. . . . It would be unfortunate if the new religion of nationalism creates a hell that burns more people than the hell of the dogmatists of yore." In Newfoundland, where laymen have had every reason to worry about their church, they knew when their loyalty was expected. "Newfoundlanders," wrote one observer, "were not a pious people. In general, they tended to take their religion as a kind of entertainment, along with their drinking and swearing and fornicating. But if they were not pious, they were ingrained sectarians, a stance that was strongly reinforced by the system of church-owned schools and inter-school athletics. . . . This and other factors fed the pervading racial conflict between British and Irish."[8]

Lay leaders are effective agents for bishops. Surely, a reader may ask, a bishop does not run public institutions or, through laymen, give orders to governments? He does not. He is rarely seen to intervene, except in vital issues into which he throws his full weight directly. But his power is such that in practice, policies and changes have to be checked with him, which means that little of importance is done or changed without anticipating his wishes. It is entertaining to watch, as I have many times, a college board member agreeing on something at one board meeting and retracting at the next after being obviously briefed by clerics. It is a nuisance that has to be tolerated too often in cabinet and caucus. And, it is a privilege that is not enjoyed by non-Catholic clergy.

This activity is not just for a church's purpose; it goes in the other direction too. Laymen interested in a career in public life will use church politics as a stepping stone to party and electoral support, and as an indication of respectability, whether they deserve it or not.

Some non-Catholic observers may point out that their churches do not have bishops, and ask if it is desirable to have ministers and elders active in public policy competing for power with Catholic bishops and politicians. On the Island at least, ministers do not have enough training and experience to do it properly. The same is true of Catholic priests, but they get briefing and marching orders from a hierarchy, ministers do not. In any event experienced politicians know the truth expressed by the eminent democrat Harry Golden: "The best advice an officeholder can get is to see that in general the ministers are not on his side."[9] They get into trouble if they are the naïve type. And they are so often wrong. Even if they mean well, as Lord Melbourne said, "the danger of religious zeal is the spirit of ill-will, hatred and malice of intolerance and persecution, which, in its own warmth and sincerity, it is too apt to engender."[10]

As for bishops, Queen Victoria was frank: "A very ugly party" she said of bishops at a Lambeth Conference. "I do not like bishops. . . . I like the man but *not* the bishop."[11] Perhaps the Vatican agrees with her, since it has expressed reservations about Conferences of Catholic Bishops. In 1988 a United States committee of Catholic bishops "rejected a draft Vatican document that calls for curtailing the role of national bishops' conferences."[12] After reading many statements of the Canadian one, my sympathy is with the Vatican.

Clerical power of Catholic bishops in every diocese is backed by old-fashioned imperialistic rulers, caparisoned in grandeur, steeped in authority, and housed in luxury at a time when most countries have cut much pomp and decoration from their governments. The Pope as pontifex maximus is an absolute monarch of the Roman model. He has a college of about 140 cardinals, elderly bachelors called "princes of the church." Each of the 3 000 or so bishops lives in a palace showing locally all the signs and ceremonies of episcopal rank. This enormous establishment is Roman in conception, organization, and operation, even though it is supposed to serve the carpenter of Nazareth.

In the administration of church policy and politics tactics are necessary, with supervision, to ensure that action relates to the abilities and weaknesses of personnel. For example, one of the standard tactics in church politics on Prince Edward Island was a favorite of Father Joseph's (p. 18). It is the "gentlemen's agreement," carried out secretly and with carefully contrived respectability among easily manoeuverable "men of good will." A well-prepared priest may make personal contact with an activist Protestant minister; a convivial bishop may entertain strategic persons at unrivalled dinner parties in his palace. A committee may be struck at the right time, with skilled priests and laymen, and manipulated ministers and elders sought out by the Catholic colleagues. The stage is then set for Richelieu's policies and Father Joseph's tactics. I have watched this operation on the Island to the point where it moves like a predictable well-oiled machine.

Non-Catholics may mistake tactics for "dialogue," a word much used in ecumenism. "Dialogue always makes sense," said the Vatican's James Cardinal Hamer at a news conference. "Dialogue is necessary not only to understand but also to persuade."[13] Protestant ministers and politicians are often in no position to persuade priests backed by a hierarchy; so they do what Bishop de Talleyrand said of the naughty Madam Grand who "always surrenders early to avoid scandal."

Another consistent church tactic is a simple pose of enormous effectiveness. The Catholic Church has acted for centuries as the underdog, the victim of any issue. Its hands are firmly in control, but in public they are spread sympathetically or deprecatingly to indicate innocence. The term "anti-Catholic" is widely used by the church against those who disagree, but the term "anti-Protestant" is almost never heard from Protestants, while "anti-Presbyterian" and "anti-Anglican" or the like would seem strange. Despite power and wealth, poverty and persecution are pleaded and any criticism or frank dialogue encounters a bland wall. Many Catholic academics, for example, defend the church by rewriting history or misusing academic principles to provide victim status. Abbé Lionel Groulx, Quebec's ecclesiastical handwringer, abused political history this way (p. 115-116). Francis Cardinal Spellman, Archbishop of New York, was the master of the deprecatory tactic.

"An aspect of Spellman's power," wrote his biographer, "was the inability of most Catholics to see criticism of the Cardinal as anything but an assault on their religion. Brought up with their defences ever ready, Catholics saw themselves as a beleaguered minority. . . . Yet Catholics had been in control of the city's politics for as long as anyone could remember . . . Catholicism was the largest and wealthiest religion in the city. It was difficult to find an area of civil life where the Church's interests weren't well-represented; yet the siege mentality persisted. One of the results was the inability of most Catholics to separate Spellman the man from the Church. Whenever he was criticized Catholics formed ranks around him; this was reflected in the business community as well as in politics."[14]

The underdog tactic may become a martyr's issue among much publicized clerics. Joseph Cardinal Mindszenty was regarded by two observers as "up to his ears in plotting inside Hungary," and "did not want to be free." And Aloysius Cardinal Stepinac whose followers "wanted him to stay in Yugoslavia as a symbol of alleged opposition to the Catholic Church by Tito" was a questionable participant in that country's troubles.

Church defensive tactics are used everywhere for offensive purposes because they will attract sympathy, rally the faithful, and appear to justify any action right or wrong. They spill over into other areas of life from school competitions to political contests to war. They encourge the cranky, bitter side of humanity. Harmony on both local and world scales is often the victim with religion taking the blame that it does not deserve.

This siege mentality has been an obvious tactic in relations between Quebec and "the rest of Canada" because it slides so easily from church to state in what is a one-church province. Quebec as the supposedly beleaguered underdog gets full publicity and sympathy, while to suggest she is an obvious beneficiary of Confederation has been a well-cultivated taboo. Her desire for appointments and patronage is so much catered to that the shares of other provinces have diminished. Indeed, even at the highest level of political power, Quebec dominates, but will not admit it and keeps asking for more. The situation is described by an exceptionally well-informed Catholic who was Canada's best-known newspaperman of his day. "We are up to our necks with Catholics in high places," wrote Charles Lynch, "Yet the country is heavy with Protestants – it's just that they don't seem to get anywhere in our politics. . . . At Government House . . . the Roman rite runs strong with three Catholic Governors General in a row [followed by a Ukrainian Greek Orthodox and a fourth Catholic]. . . . Of the 20 most senior members of the federal cabinet, 14 are Roman Catholics – ten francophones."[15]

Since 1968 five out of the six prime ministers have been Catholics, the three-month term of Ms. Campbell being the exception, and their presently apparent successors will continue the trend. "It is at least curious," continued Mr. Lynch, "that . . . Roman Catholics have become so prominent in the federal power structure – more prominent, in fact, than in any other country with a Protestant majority."

Mr. Lynch's view was supported ten years later by Jeffrey Simpson. He observed how "without the rest of Canada noticing, the government is structured with Quebecers or fancophones almost everywhere at the top: Prime Minister, Minister of Finance, Minister of Foreign Affairs, Minister of Inter-governmental Affairs, chief of staff, principal secretary, clerk and deputy clerk of the Privy Council, govenor general to be [and the Chief Justice of Canada and the Speaker of both houses of Parliament]."[16] It is also "curious" and "without the rest of Canada noticing," both Quebec and federal governments are dominated by fancophone and Roman Catholic officials on both sides of discussion about the future of Canada, and English Canada is urged not to ask questions of Quebec. This arrangement is worthy of Cardinal Richelieu's politics, a natural result of the expulsion of Protestant Huguenots from Quebec, and, as we shall see (p. 115) a tactic favorable to Abbé Lionel Groulx's ambitions for a "racially pure French Catholic state within or without . . . Confederation."[17]

How such situations are implemented with long-term church planning is illustrated in a personal experience I had as a member of the Royal Commission on Electoral Reform on the Island in 1961. For many years 15 constituencies, now 16, sent two members each to the provincial Legislature. There were two reasons for these two-member districts. Thirty single ones would be too small in size and population. And the Catholic minority supported the practice of having Catholic against Catholic and Protestant against Protestant in each district when desired, thus ensuring one from each faith in the House and avoiding religious voting conflicts. However, as the Protestant majority in the population changed to a Catholic one, this procedure was criticized for being out of date. Straight contests became favored, without the obvious question asked: would Catholics now be able to secure huge majorities in the House which the Protestants were hitherto prevented from attaining?

The chairman of the Royal Commission of 1961, Judge Sylvere DesRoches, advocated the change to single constituencies. I put forward two arguments. Change should be brought about by cutting the size of the House in half; thirty tiny constituencies would have backyard politics. And the Commission should give thought to the implications of denominational division planned for the Catholic minority being withdrawn for a Protestant minority. The Commission decided to leave the questions unanswered. Judge DesRoches was not amused. Now, however, the subject is being discussed again with another Commission. The two questions are still relevant; whether they will be answered and what will be the result remain to be seen.

Many features of church politics on the Island could have been changed at Confederation. Had the Island been joined with the small neighboring provinces in the 1860s, as the Maritime Fathers of Confederation originally discussed, a plan which was the reason for their 1864 Conference, and had the three entered Canada together as one substantial province, the future might have been kinder. But that opportunity passed them by. It was almost inevitable, therefore, that the very small Island was turned into a church fantasy land following the ecclesiastical aggrandizement of the colonial years. The political power lies exclusively with the Roman Catholic Church, and what it will agree to pretty well determines social and political policy. For weakness the Island's Protestant churches seem unrivalled. There has been no recognizable potentate among non-Catholic clergy, not even one clerical statesman who lent personal presence and effectiveness to a public issue. I have never heard of a minister who could cause a flutter in a premier's office. And I doubt if there is an official with more pathetic status than the President of the Ministerial Association; few are aware that there is one; and almost nobody knows his name.

This imbalance of power is not a happy state of affairs, and it turns local troubles like temperance, divorce, and abortion into bitter political crises. As an expert said of the issues of Louis Riel's Manitoba, "Roman Catholic and Anglican clergy reinforced existing divisions. . . . Clerics induced meddling and gossip [and] sparked public scandals."[18] These words, which also describe some developments in Canada's North, fit perfectly many of the Island's social issues, particularly those that were badly mauled by the Island churches in 1945 when the war's end required change.

For wielding power on the local level on the Island the Bishop enjoys complete coverage throughout the province for his information and instructions by means of a motley bevy of men with tenure, time, and comfortable living to do the exclusive duties of the church. During the university issue, with 75 to 80 priests and many nuns in the tiny diocese, the Bishop's wishes, plus current gossip, could spread easily to every parish. Non-Catholics have no such network; they cannot get or give out organized information; and there is no central prestigious official to whom they may send their views on public issues, or through whom they may take effective common action or make adequate representation to authorities. The head offices of Protestant ministers are not impressive, and their primates and moderators only serve for short terms.

On the Catholic side clergy provide a special problem – they are all bachelors. It is easy to say that they are wedded to the church, and to think they should devote their entire lives to it. But a world organization is motivated and managed by a consolidation of half a million or so bachelors? On the Island the impacts of several dozen strategically placed full-time bachelors on church politics is strong in the communities. There is of course nothing wrong with being unmarried, but for a huge profession to make a theoretical fetish of it may cultivate in priests many of the attitudes of those who like to appear as guardians of alleged virtue and devotees of narrow experience. And all ages are involved; there are some "old fogeys," and "young fogeys" too. With no family responsibility they have much time and inclination for church politics. This subject is now being examined throughout the church in connection with married priests and ordination of women. Mass bachelorhood as a force in church politics should be included in the discussion.

A large part of Island church politics and tactics concerns church patronage. Patronage is of course to be found in all governments. But in small places it becomes dominant because appointees depend on it for status as well as jobs, and powerful groups are in a position to make the most of it. Recently, in 1993, two doctors gave remarkable testimony. One, Dr. Herb Dickieson, member of an Island task force on education, reported that "M.L.A.s rule Islanders through the most endemic and penetrating system of political patronage anywhere in Canada. . . . Islanders must work together to shed the yoke of political patronage and press politicians to end this morally bankrupt practice."[19] A former minister, Dr. L.G. Dewar, gave a detailed public account of his own search for personal patronage in an essay on *Gubernatorial Aspirations,* which is a unique description of this political game.[20]

A *Guardian* editorial of February 8, 1995 noted that "patronage is regarded by many as a prerequisite of the very political Island Way of Life;" but it is "also a lousy way to run a government. . . . It costs too much because for a political party to maintain a system of patronage, it has to maintain a body of work that exists primarily as a reward for party faithful, and not give the Canadian taxpayer value for money."

Only a quarter of prospective patronage appointees are considered when the two-party and two-church affiliations are recognized, and thus the chances are that successful candidates are weak ones. Politicians on both sides agree with this view – when they are in opposition. Church people often aggravate the situation by suggesting the "turn," now one side, next the other. Catholics tried for years to get that practice adopted at Prince of Wales. On the whole,

political and church patronage appointments on the Island have been mediocre, unfair, or bad, not because the appointees belonged to a particular group,
but because their affiliation was all that qualified them for selection. And they
continued unsuitable when they could rely on their group to protect them from
dismissal or get themselves undeserved promotion. Indeed, patronage blocks
the advancement of many able career civil servants that have the personal
qualifications.

Just after I went to Charlottetown, Premier Jones and Bishop James Boyle
exchanged views on patronage. Bishop Boyle wrote to Jones on July 16, 1949
complaining that Catholics comprised 40-50 per cent of the population, but
that there were no Catholic ministers without portfolio in the government. The
Premier replied that if the Catholics wanted to be represented in the Cabinet
they should elect better M.L.A.s that he would wish to appoint. Mr. Jones also
believed that Catholic ministers acted on the basis of ecclesiastical directives
rather than on cabinet solidarity and a premier's leadership (he told me he said
that to the Bishop too). In a lively exchange in the Legislature, a prominent
layman, W.J.P. Macmillan, asked Jones why he went off the Island for a Prince
of Wales principal. "Why," Jones shot back, "does your church always go off
the Island for its Bishop?"[21]

Some Island politicians are aware of patronage and try to do something
about it. When I was discussing with Provincial Secretary David Stewart
prospective nominees for appointments to the boards of the College and the
Confederation Centre, he told me the hardest job in cabinet was to find enough
able people from the small population to go around for the many offices and
institutions. When government was lumbering along in a particularly notice-
able way in 1964, Mr. Stewart, a Conservative, told the Legislature that "we
have a cabinet of eight and a presiding officer [it is ten now]. Too large, too
cumbersome, too voluble – the same as this House [laughter] – too many
squeaking wheels. Let us be sensible for goodness sake. Let us get down to
size; let us cut this unwieldy thing to a workable size." "This," replied
Opposition Leader and former Premier A.W. Matheson, a Liberal, "is good,
solid advice."[22]

The second form of patronage is in the supply of goods and services. The
virtues of competition and tendering are honored more in the breach than in
the observance, and the Island pays from a quarter to a third more for what it
builds or buys. Indeed, the most costly and inefficient document in government is the patronage list.

Like all Islanders, I knew about patronage when I went to the province. But
I was not prepared for the extent of it, or for examples of it at Prince of Wales.
The faculty was splendid, but there was a handful of political and church

appointees who were inadequate, and poor advertisements for the College. Before I was appointed was the time to get this subject on the official table. I spoke to Premier Jones about it and he agreed. Indeed, he told me of a particularly unsatisfactory faculty member and offered to fire him before I was appointed, saying the man was trouble and it was only church patronage that put him in the College years before. This was a surprise, but I thought the Premier's offer a bad precedent, especially since I was at that very moment president of the Faculty Club at Carleton in Ottawa, and interested in academic freedom. I declined the offer and later regretted it because the person continued to be incompetent.

It was not enough to rely on the Premier's support of my views on patronage. I needed the backing of the Cabinet. At a meeting with a majority of the ministers I requested there be no political or church patronage at Prince of Wales and gave them my reasons. They agreed and we never had to accept a patronage appointment thenceforth. But some strategically placed people never forgave or forgot.

A reader may wonder at my attitude to church politics and ask what happened to encourage it. I encountered many sad events growing up in a divided school system and read of many more in my research on the Island. But several issues around the beginning of my years at the College illustrate how church action can put an official on guard and keep his skepticism active.

The first event was described to me in detail three years before I went to the Island. I was teaching at Carleton, whose founding president was Dr. Henry Marshal Tory, Canada's leading educational statesman of his day. He had been a founder of four universities and the National Research Council, and he had been one of the McGill professors handling the Macdonald/McGill/Prince of Wales business of 1906-7. He and a group of Ottawa business and professional men applied to the Ontario Legislature for an act incorporating Carleton College as a university. A well-organized opposition was led by James Cardinal McGuigan, Archbishop of Toronto, designed to preserve the monopoly of the Catholic University of Ottawa. It was supported by some at Queen's, McGill, and the University of Toronto, as well as by Mayor Charlotte Whitton of Ottawa, a close friend of the bishop of that city.[23] It is interesting to note that the Cardinal, an Islander, had graduated from Prince of Wales as winner of the Governor General's medal, and as a priest was secretary to Bishop Henry O'Leary who had piloted St. Dunstan's incorporation through the Legislature.

I saw Dr. Tory frequently and he told me much of what had gone on. The Cardinal had lobbied personally and through colleagues and laymen in nearby universities, and had frightened members of the Legislature. The politicians did not approve the proposed bill, but later they did incorporate Carleton, not under the Universities Act, but under the Companies Act. It was given the name "The Ottawa Institute for the Advancement of Learning," by which it was known until opposition died down.

Another incident preceded a visit of the then Princess Elizabeth and the Duke of Edinburgh in 1951 and provoked a silly public squabble between the Rector of St. Paul's, Charlottetown, and Premier Jones. The Rector was angry about the seating of head table guests at the state dinner, maintaining that a minister of the visitors' church should be at the head table in addition to the Bishop and the President of the Ministerial Association. The Premier refused; protocol made no such provision. A long series of letters by Premier and rector to newspapers was an undignified display of misjudged public relations.[24]

Two years later there occurred the only Catholic complaint to me about religious affiliation. An I.O.D.E. scholarship committee, of which I was a member, selected a winner with whom everyone was satisfied. Next morning an active church layman and father of another candidate made an almost insane display of anger about his son being passed over because he was a Catholic. I told him church affiliation had not been involved and referred him to the chairman. He promised dire consequences.

About the same time, what amounted to attempted robbery disturbed financial relations at Prince of Wales. The federal government had arranged its grants to the universities, and we at Prince of Wales were advised from Ottawa that we were eligible because we had two university years. The Principal-elect of Queen's University was to be installed on October 20, 1951, and I had been unable to accept an invitation to the ceremony. However, I was telephoned from Kingston by the President of the University of New Brunswick telling me that Catholic pressure was being applied individually to prominent guests advocating that all the Island share of the grants should go to St. Dunstan's. I must, he said, come to Kingston immediately to make appropriate contacts with strategic guests who could do something about the situation. I took the first plane, spent a profitable few days, and was assured by sympathetic promises of help. Prince of Wales got the grants.

Pandemonium then broke out in the halls of the Island's Legislature as a Knight of St. Gregory charged at various government offices. There followed a spectacular combination of inquisition and comic opera which would have made a great subject for a play by Hal Roach or Gilbert and Sullivan.

On stage was Dr. W.J.P. Macmillan, who had long crusaded in Island politics. He was a bright, imposing, but strangely egotistical man, a respected doctor who had won a gold medal in medical school. His church had recognized him with a papal knighthood. But nature played him a sad trick when she allowed him to think he was a politician.

Dr. Macmillan had been in and out of Premier Jones's office for several years complaining about Prince of Wales. Before my predecessor retired he asked the Premier to give a Catholic a turn at the job. He opposed my appointment and protested every change that was made, and especially the federal grants for the College. He early learned my views on patronage when he asked me to intercede at McGill for a friend of his who was refused admission to its medical school. I declined for obvious reasons.

The Doctor had been a "loose canon" as a minister in the J.D. Stewart government with a limited respect for collegiality among colleagues. Mrs. S.N. Robertson, the widow of one of my predecessors told me much about the Doctor's inclination to interfere. He had frequently dropped in on Dr. Robertson with requests to admit or pass students or provide some patronage.

Macmillan succeeded Premier Stewart in 1933. In the subsequent general election of 1935 he and his party lost every seat in the Legislature. Unfortunately for his own party (the Conservatives) he hung on to the leadership during two decades of opposition and, upon being pushed out, he kept active and talkative, paid no attention to party collegiality and helped ruin the career of his successor, R.R. Bell, by undermining his authority. Premier Jones took full advantage of Macmillan by encouraging him in his mistakes and playing him off against Mr. Bell. Jones said of the Doctor that, although a Conservative, he was the "best friend the Liberals ever had" because he kept them in office for 26 years.

The early 1950s were the McCarthy era in the United States. Everyone knows the shame the Senator caused a whole generation by his inquisitions, and by his success in hoodwinking sensible citizens. The Doctor also had a well-known Canadian precedent for such persecution by a Catholic layman in a legislature. The victim was President Henry Thornton of the Canadian National Railways; the inquisitor was John T. Hackett, member of the House of Commons for Stanstead, Quebec. The grilling of Thornton in a parliamentary committee was so vicious that the press dubbed it "Hackett's racket," and students of public administration wondered for years why Parliament had allowed it in a democracy that had due process of law.[25] Every tactic of the McCarthy and Hackett affairs was adopted by Macmillan.

Dr. Macmillan said much about the College and me in the House without asking for information beforehand.[26] I thought all this one-sided and asked Premier A.W. Matheson to request the House to receive me in committee. He agreed and so did other party leaders on both sides. Macmillan was furious.

But members had been developing considerable disgust with the Doctor. He was not being fair in his comments about the College or me. And when Walter Jones retired to the Senate, and members were paying him the usual tributes, Macmillan declared that it was a "fortunate thing" for the Province that Jones had gone, and press and public reacted with anger.[27]

Upon my arrival at the House several members of both parties told me to "give him Hell." There was nothing I would have liked better to do; and M.L.A.s themselves would have done it long before if they had dared. But it would be self-defeating for a witness to pluck the feathers of a Knight of St. Gregory in the Island Legislature; so I just ruffled them a bit. The Doctor proposed no courtesy; when I passed him accidentally in the House the first morning he grunted "Hello, prisoner at the bar."

The legislative chamber and gallery were packed on March 24, 1954. I was asked to make some preliminary remarks and I devoted these to answering what the Doctor had said. Thenceforth I used replies to questions to give information, thus avoiding some dangerous features of inquisitions by assuring members that they, not the questioner, were in control of the agenda and the answers were for them. This tactic greatly annoyed Macmillan who was desperately trying to lure me into an argument with him on his terms. He adopted the easy but unfair tactic followed by inquisitions of condemning me personally for whatever he had to complain about. He growled provocations. "Do you teach political science at Prince of Wales?" he demanded. "Yes." "Does St. Dunstan's teach political science?" "No." "Then I suggest you cut it out." Whereupon he drew a roar of laughter from the gallery when he suggested students learn political science by visiting the Legislature.

I thought things went well, and so did many members who spoke to me afterward.[28] The press published the proceedings. The next day Ralph Cameron, legislative reporter for both Charlottetown papers, told me that Dr. Macmillan had visited the papers in high dudgeon and objected to him and his editors about the large amount of coverage of my remarks. He wanted this generosity stopped, which request naturally prompted the papers to continue reporting.[29]

As the proceedings rolled on it was apparent that Macmillan would not accept a fact or opinion that opposed his views or explained the educational situation. He even asked the Speaker to require Mr. Bell, his own leader, to withdraw remarks he made in support of Prince of Wales.[30] This got tiresome and many members complained, including ministers. A "damn waste of time," a Liberal called it on the floor; "with no justification" added a Conservative. And a cabinet minister told the House that he "wants Prince of Wales left alone."[31] Indeed, the Premier, who knew everything that had gone on at the

College, believed that things were going too well to suit the Doctor and his church. When a draft report of the committee came before the House, both sides, including committee members, tackled it with gusto and voted out what were obviously the Doctor's comments critical of Prince of Wales and me.[32] They no doubt agreed with a local education authority that Macmillan's "lack of regard for public testimony given under oath indicates only disrespect for the truth and fair play."[33]

At the end of this episode several members of the House spoke to me about an old Island problem that we have seen in earlier pages. Catholics were much interested in the Macmillan affair; but, with only one exception, not a word of support for Prince of Wales or me came from non-Catholic clergy and elders. A similar situation had appeared in the McCarthy and Hackett affairs. This was a bitter complaint of Premiers Jones and Matheson – that Protestants natter about trifles like seating at head tables and having church ladies take the names of their members entering the liquor store. (Yes, they actually did it; having heard of it I went to the store and saw it with astonishment.) But in times of crisis, while Catholics talk and act, Protestant ministers and elders often refuse to stand up and be counted. When facing Richelieu dominance Protestants did not display Luther courage, and tragedy followed their neglect.

The biggest problem behind Macmillan's attempted pogrom was that Prince of Wales lacked a board of govenors. As we have noted, it was Premier W.W. Sullivan, another papal knight, who abolished the board, leaving the College defenceless against any church critic or meddler who came along, and making it more difficult for the College to be administered. Criticism is of course important for any college, but church criticism is usually launched irresponsibly and unfairly and accompanied by accusations of wrong doing and assumed virtue that make it almost impossible to answer the critics. Dr. Macmillan must have known that the lack of a board had killed the Macdonald/McGill/Prince of Wales proposal, and that by 1954 no other college or university was in this position. Yet he told the Legislature that my desire for a board was an attempt to usurp powers of the Cabinet itself.

I gave the House the reasons for having a suitable board of governors for Prince of Wales, and they were published verbatim in the press.[34] This was the first time the members heard of them, and the House gave us a new board that year as a result. I include them here because they stimulated opposition from Macmillan and other church members, and illustrate why the board was needed.

1. Puts authority in the hands of persons who have a direct, separate, and sympathetic interest in the institution.

2. Ensures better management because there is direct contact at all times between those who decide policy and those who carry it out.

3. Ensures full responsibility to the legislature and cabinet yet avoids or limits the danger of undue political or other pressure.

4. Provides far more responsiveness to public opinion and at the same time provides protection against selfish interests who prefer to work behind the scenes rather than in the open.

5. Avoids the lethargy, bureaucracy, and red tape which always results from departmental control of a non-departmental function. Control of educational institutions by departments of education has always failed and it has been abolished practically everywhere in Canada.

6. Avoids the drastic and upsetting changes which may result from changes of governments and ministers.

7. Provides for the running of the institution on a business as well as an educational basis. Business efficiency should always accompany public control.

8. Provides for the receiving of gifts and grants, and the proper saving and investment of moneys. This can only be done if the accounts of the institution are placed under proper business management and in an account separate from the public consolidated revenue.

9. Provides for full functional and financial accounting to the legislature and government.

10. Takes advantage of the fact that the public respects such an institution far more than one which is under direct political control.

11. Such a system is now used in practically every publicly-owned institution in Canada.

All these reasons were elementary to anyone familiar with post-secondary education in the 1950s. But they were unknown in Prince Edward Island because of its government's neglect of modern public administration and the church's desire to sustain control. Other academic practices were equally unknown. These, taken for granted elsewhere, were: non-political appointments, faculty councils, academic freedom, sabbaticals, compulsory retirement at 65, leaves of absence and retirement to enter politics, business management, research, public relations in other activities besides sport, and separation from patronage and church politics. I introduced all these to Prince of Wales College and was heavily criticized for each one by our diocesan opposition. Yet they were met by most politicians with reasonable discussion leading to agreement and implementation. Furthermore, when the University of Prince Edward Island began it did not have to fight again for these principles – a legacy from Prince of Wales alone.

While the Macmillan affair was starting, a New Brunswick event illustrated a very different and sensible approach to relations between government and higher education – exactly what we needed at Prince of Wales.

When Premier John B. McNair took office he resigned as a member of the Senate of the University of New Brunswick. "Solely," he wrote U.N.B.'s President, "with the thought of removing all further opportunities for misunderstanding and that nothing be permitted . . . to interfere with the work of the Senate and those who, under it, are responsible for the active management of the affairs of the University, I have decided to disassociated myself from its administration. . . . I have valued greatly my association with the Senate. . . . During the years I have been connected with it no single incident has occurred to suggest anything of a political nature in the administration of the University affairs. I know that this happy condition will continue."[35]

"This happy condition" was a feature of U.N.B.'s success. It and Prince of Wales began as similar public institutions under similar circumstances. But, even with nearby Catholic colleges in New Brunswick, no unions were forced, and the publicly-owned college was allowed to develop into a university because its board of governors and men like McNair took an interest in it and protected it against church aggression.

There was a difficult consequence of the Macmillan affair for me. On P.E.I. the "dear souls" types never understood the Bishops and clerics as politicians; a Knight of St. Gregory made a big impression in a tiny place. The "small c" conservatives did not want to be disturbed; political workers cherished their patronage; politicians found debate on church politics upsetting; and the ecumenists tut-tutted about everybody being brothers. As was their habit when disturbed, clergy looked for a scapegoat. Accordingly, I was, they said, bringing too many new-fangled ideas and people from outside, and doing too much to upset local church attitudes even though the church had raised most of the complaints. I had been doing what I was supposed to do, at all times with the consent of the government and, when it was established, the Board of Governors, and after full consultation and discussion in the faculty. The need was great, and changes had to be made quickly because the Catholic opposition was bullish and the Protestant clergy were cowed. Furthermore, church critics made no effort to analyze the changes at the College, let alone prove them wrong. They just attacked as they had for a century and a half.

Fortunately, I had maximum cooperation from the Prince of Wales faculty and, except for one Catholic layman and one non-Catholic self-promoter, we worked as a team for the College. When the criticism got personal and rough almost all of them, from every discipline, age group and church affiliation, initiated and signed a statement dated April 11, 1968. "We," they said, "the undersigned members of the faculty of Prince of Wales College, believe that Dr. Frank MacKinnon has attempted to create at the College a unique and superior educational program, and that there are already manifest signs of success. We wish to assert our confidence in him."

There was another, and more surprising, expression of confidence – from the Bishop himself! I had actually a friendly social relationship with Bishop Malcolm MacEachern, as two Scots with much in common. I dined happily once a year at his palace. He and his nuns set a magnificent table; his cocktails, which he made himself, were by far the best and strongest served in Charlotte-town, and excellent conversation flourished with the memorable meals. I liked him as a person, but the heritage of Scots does include clan rivalry.

I received one day from Lieutenant-Governor W.J. MacDonald an invitation to have tea with him. I knew him well because he had been on our faculty for many years. We had a good time over the teacups, he obviously having something to say, and I wondering what it was. Finally he rang for the butler who, upon instructions, brought for me two bottles of Montbasillac wine, a grand dinner favorite with the Bishop and me, and a communion wine used at the Basilica. The Governor told me the Bishop had asked him to give me the wine and a message. The Bishop offered to nominate me as president if I would agree to a union of St. Dunstan's and Prince of Wales as one university. I asked the Governor to send back my thanks to the Bishop for his wine and message. And I said I would be glad to sit down with him after Prince of Wales had time to complete its arrangements upon receiving university status. Then we could carry out one of the normal plans used occasionally elsewhere for cooperation among public and church colleges.

I thought this a fair reply. After all, it was obvious that we at Prince of Wales could not play bridge without a share of the face cards, and with the opponents' "kibbitzers" standing back of us, and the Bishop keeping score. Indeed it was not the Bishop's business to make such a deal; and he must have known, as I did, that it was not my business either. If and when the time came, the initiative for a presidential appointment was the prerogative of the Board of Governors, and the acceptance of a Bishop's advance conditional nomination would be a dangerous precedent. Perhaps if he had agreed with my reply, and we had met a year or two later for a weekend with a good cook and a case of Montbasillac on hand, we might have devised a sensible plan. But it was not to be; there was by this time too much clerical and political flotsam and jetsam that had to be cleaned up.

Chapter Seven

THE MARCH OF FOLLY

A revived demand for university status for Prince of Wales followed the Macmillan crusade. The last one had faded with the end of the Macdonald/Mc-Gill/Prince of Wales plan in 1907. Alumni and friends were now asking about it again. Educationists were enquiring in view of rising enrollments and the need for the College's two extra years in Eastern Canada. Now taxpayers were funding the expansion of no less than eight Maritime Catholic colleges through federal and provincial grants, and there was no move to unite any of them. When was Prince of Wales to get its opportunity? And how was it to cope with the sectarian danger?

At this time Prince of Wales was getting a splendid new neighbor, and culture was about to enter the Island with great impact. Circumstances combined to give me the opportunity to propose and carry out a cultural centre project to honor the Fathers of Confederation on the centennial of their first meeting in Charlottetown in 1864. I worked at it alone for several years, with the government's knowledge and consent, and with public skepticism. "It won't work, but you can try it," said Premier Matheson. In due course, a foundation of volunteer national directors, of which I was president, incorpo-rated itself to do the job; the governments of Canada and the provinces agreed to pay the cost and gave the foundation a completely free hand. Competitions and tenders were used for all construction and services; patronage was avoided; there was no deficit or over-run; and a combined theatre, art gallery, museum, library and memorial hall went up in time for the Queen to open it in 1964. The cost was $5.6 million in 1964 dollars. Soon the place hummed with activity and the Centre's festivals and exhibitions brought all kinds of Canadian culture to the Island. This the Island got for nothing; its contribution was the site. And shortly after the opening the federal government agreed to the foundation's request for an annual $250 000 which was then adequate for operation and maintenance.[1]

The relevance of Confederation Centre to Prince of Wales College was direct and enormous. They were two blocks apart. The College had taken over some nearby buildings; a new residence was built and another planned; property was already bought, and more agreed upon, for nearby playing fields;

and expansion was to carry the campus through to Prince Street, near the Confederation Centre. An experienced architect, who had worked on Scarborough's campus in Toronto and won our competition, made appropriate models and plans which impressed the Board of Governors, faculty, and government. The cost of all this was well in hand. As for Charlottetown, the Prince of Wales campus combined with the Confederation Centre would have revitalized the City's east and centre and turned it into one of those beautiful college towns so beloved in the eastern United States.

The Centre did not escape obstruction, however, which was of a similar kind experienced by the College. We had many well-organized complaints about the lack of patronage, and bringing in people "from away" who had won the competitions. And cultural activists, as always, could not agree among themselves on anything when consulted. But the most persistent burrowing beneath our efforts was by churchmen who seemed to worry that the success of the Centre would be matched at the College, which it showed every sign of doing. Right at the start the government was asked to take back its permission for the project on the ground that there already existed the Basilica Recreation Centre which would serve the purpose. That idea was easily disposed of. But when construction was about to start a Catholic cabinet minister proposed to the government that it should only permit construction if the Centre was built out of town next to St. Dunstan's.

This idea should have been killed immediately for the obstructionist and impractical tactic it obviously was. But it upset Premier Shaw into waffling, so I called a meeting of the Centre's board in Charlottetown with the Premier, the Catholic cabinet members, and some other colleagues present. After a nervous beginning Mr. Shaw put the proposal on the table. A stunned silenced resulted. Whereupon D.B. Weldon, a prominent businessman from London, Ontario, to whom we had given the task of replying, looked at the Premier with a ferocious stare. He said, in effect, "if that's what the government insists on after its previous agreements with us, so be it. But we will withdraw immediately, no Centre will be built, and the money will be returned to the federal and provincial governments with the reason why. The scandal will make the Island a laughing-stock across Canada, unless the building is put where it belongs on the agreed site next to the historic Provincial Building where the Fathers met." We had never seen anyone collapse so quickly as Shaw did then. He signed another agreement and passed an order-in-Council through the Cabinet which we insisted on in case another church political kite was put aloft. But the Centre's board members were deeply depressed by the shoddy performance.

All this was the College situation as the 1960s began. The new Board of Governors approved every project and change. We explained the plans to the government open and above board, in full view of the public. Excellent faculty had just been appointed, and others were about to come. We had the closest cooperation and valuable advice from colleagues and universities across the country. Indeed, 5 000 professors came in 1964 and were hosted and accommodated at Prince of Wales for the biggest convention the Island had seen, the Learned Societies, and so many of them liked what they saw.

But the Bishop and his associates said no, and the church politics proceeded to send the Island deeper into its role as a land of lost opportunity.

Before looking into the unbelievable details we should ask how such a thing could happen in a modern democratic society, especially when there was no reason for it. Church politics were overwhelming in the small province. Strong Catholicism and weak Protestantism had always been involved. The Island's big political engine crammed into a small body had been consistently in disarray. But something else, new and unexpected, appeared to exaggerate these problems in the last dangerous years. Islanders abjectly surrendered to what was mistakenly called "ecumenism."

Ecumenism, the idea of one universal Christian church, is a highly controversial dogmatic theological concept. Its discussants of the 1960s had been irreconcilable – on the one hand an authoritarian clerical regime with everyone in step, and on the other hand varying groups worshiping and serving God in their own ways.

The possibilities for ecumenism were always prevented by church politics. There was some hope when negotiations between Catholics and Anglicans were authorized by Pope Paul VI in 1966, although some members of the hierarchy were warning against too much optimism; Cardinal Hume of Westminster, for example, spoke of "conversion." But whatever ecumenists thought, reported *Time*, they later had to "contend with" John Paul II who persisted in "centralizing and strengthening papal authority, rather than moving in a direction that would attract Anglicans." An ecumenical agreement was reached but it collapsed. "Rather than endorse the painstakingly crafted agreement, the Vatican issued a statement insisting that a reunited church must be built upon a papacy that is a God-given 'permanent' institution with 'universal' jurisdiction, 'directly founded' by Jesus Christ. The text also reasserts the Pope's personal power to teach infallibility on faith and morals."[2] Said the Archbishop of Canterbury, with marked understatement, "As ecumenists search the rubble for bits of optimism further progress will be hazardous."[3]

Despite the warnings and failures, many non-Catholics were persuaded, against all the evidence and despite the Pope's pronouncements, that ecumenism was right and the will of God. They included too many of those who think undisciplined theology with the vocabulary of dreams. They were not prepared to study the record or to tolerate the views of others who dared to disagree with them. As for the record, it seemed clear everywhere for a long time. "If one religion only were allowed in England," wrote Voltaire, "the government would very possibly become arbitrary; if there are but two, the people would cut one another's throats; but as there is such a multitude, they all live happy and in peace."[4]

"The cry for orthodoxy became the most furious and implacable of all human passions," wrote David Hume, "merit and salvation were more and more divorced from virtue and attached to ritual observance and unquestioning belief . . . the life of man was tarnished with lip service and insincerity."[5] The power of hate and its entrenched position in man's personality, including his church behavior, are well-known phenomena, and they are to be seen today in the "politically correct" movement. The tragedy of forced one-direction union was played out in Ireland and Korea where all the evidence indicated that leaving existing boundaries alone would be the happiest and best solution, saving countless lives.

These world-scale views were reflected in the politics of Canada. "Social peace," reported James Stewart, editorial writer of the *Montreal Gazette* in *Macleans*, "is the phrase Bourassa uses to explain that he can't be too nice to English-speaking Quebecers for fear of inciting francophones to riot . . . trimming public policy to suit the brick-throwers and spray-can artists."[6] On the Island this approach was to become "we can't be too nice to Prince of Wales for fear of inciting the Catholics." In both provinces the approach was in one direction only.

The problems of ecumenism were explained in a published brochure in 1964 by Rev. Scarth Macdonnell of Stanley Presbyterian Church, Westmount, Quebec. "It is," he wrote, "an observable fact that the formation of large ecclesiastical unities results in the depersonalization of Christian people. . . . It is characteristic of degenerate Christians to submerge their identity, and to hide in big congregations."[7] The dominating attitude of supporters of ecumenism is, to me who was bombarded by it, well described by Mr. Macdonnell. "If you are not to-day committed to the ecumenical principle of 'striving for unity,' you are regarded as a theological eccentric and an ecclesiastical pariah" motivated by a "guilty conscience," "bigotry," and "self-interest." He cited a church working paper entitled *Presbyterians and the Church Catholic* as saying that "we all confess that simple self-will operates to keep us separated." Strange, I would have thought it was common sense that did it, in view of the church politics involved.

On Prince Edward Island, the ecumenical allegations of virtue and sin were assembled in the university question. When English Anglicans were hoping, the Charlottetown clergy were agog. Macdonnell's message, supported by historian Rev. Stanford Reid of McGill University (who was well known on the Island) was ignored by Island ministers. At almost the very moment the Pope authorized discussion Island Catholics marshalled the ecumenists, and then scattered them when the Pope withdrew his assurances and Prince of Wales was gone. The historic circle was thus completed; what Richelieu did in Paris and Canada determined the history of Island education; and now what John Paul II did in Rome was decisive in forcing its direction.

Charlottetown's Catholic clergy were using a famous tactic. They made ecumenism a Trojan Horse. The Protestant clergy and laymen, like the Trojans, were lulled into receiving the alleged gift and never knew what was happening to them, although they had been warned of danger. The victim was now Prince of Wales and by the time the doomed ecumenical movement had served its purpose and was killed by the Pope it was too late to repair the damage.

The victim status of the College was important to both sides. Before ecumenism it was an unprotected pawn in the struggle between church and state. But during the movement it was turned into a symbol, a sacrificial offering if necessary, for an alleged coming together of Island Christendom and a washing away of the "sin" of separation. For Catholics this was a front for tactics. For non-Catholic clergy and laymen – as we shall see, carefully selected and cultivated by Catholics for ecumenical relations – it served as a crusade which became little more than a PR stunt for naïve unprepared activists. And the Protestant ministers never thought to ask how ecumenism could be combined with the separate school approach. They never realized who the winners and losers would be.

An old and widespread church tactic was shunning, and it created another victim – me. Catholics and selected non-Catholic clergy and laymen followed the traditional procedure of blaming, not an institution, but a representative villain in it for any complaint that could be conveniently found. Before 1962 participants in the issue ranged a bit in discussions. After that the word went out. Confirmed later in a letter written by the Bishop to his priests, it was stated that I was acting alone and should be blamed for the lack of one-way progress. The critics never blamed the College Board, the Citizens' Committee, the Royal Commission on Higher Education, or the government for their consenting parts in the project. This new use of a characteristic church tactic prevented any real dialogue in Charlottetown. What was new about it to me, who was trying to save the College, was the way ecumenists avoided me like the plague. They would only listen to what they wanted to hear – exactly as Reverend Scarth Macdonnell described it.

An Island newspaper reported accurately on my dilemma. "Intelligent criticism," it said, "is necessary in any healthy democratic society. . . . All of MacKinnon's interpretations of Island politics are, of course, open to debate. His critics might be able to prove him wrong. But the point is that they are simply not trying. Instead they are attacking. . . . That in itself shows all is not well with the P.E.I. body politic."[8] I would only add that the clerical opinion, Catholic and Protestant, was never open to real two-way discussion throughout the entire crisis.

Despite ecumenism, the Island government did listen to us; there was widespread support for Prince of Wales; and the College got its university status from the Legislature in 1964. Nevertheless, even then, clerical piracy attacked and succeeded, but only by a whisker. We at the College thought this putsch was a breach of Christian ethics; so did many politicians that tried to help us; and I was told by unimpeachable authority, so did many Catholics who had contempt for their manipulated Protestant allies. When ecumenism did decline, all that remained were some mixed marriages and the occasional joint service which were used by ministers to keep up appearances.

Was "ecumenism" in this commotion really ecumenical? The answer from Rome and Charlottetown had to be "No," it was simply a tactic. The eminent Catholic writer Paul Johnson described ecumenism as "the Catholic Restoration" which, wrote one observer, "obviously means the end of ecumenism, except possibly with the Orthodox."[9] A few years later even the Orthodox were disillusioned. Russian, Greek and Bulgarian Orthodox complained that Catholics from western Europe, the United States and other countries pushed in where religious freedom had been recognized, and acted "as if they were moving into old mission areas where there are no believers."[10] This was the situation on Prince Edward Island too; it has always allowed itself to be treated as an old mission area and thus severely limited its own religious freedom. As a result, to use the words of Rabbi Abraham Feinberg in another connection, "the tides of human energy beat on other shores" than the Island, where "organized religion [became] full of material splendor, but dead."[11]

Where that material splendor was leading was widely suggested in Europe. A survey from Warsaw brought together fears from many countries that ecumenism was regarded as conquest. "A united Europe," declared the Pope, "has a profound cultural, spiritual and moral dimension. Christianity is at the very roots of European culture." "He wants to be the shepherd of a new

Europe," said the survey. This ambition is widely repudiated by Europe's numerous Muslims and Jews as well as many Christians. The Swiss theologian Hans Kung cites the Pope's "double standard" and describes the Vatican as "Europe's last absolutist state – an ancient regime that may publicly demand human rights of others but in its own sphere gags the freedom of conscience of the press and of opinion."[12] It is the view of ecumenism as conquest that helped its decline. This Prince Edward Island never understood, because there Hans Kung's observation applied, freedom of conscience was gagged, and ecumenism was conquest carefully disguised. And Bishop MacEachern seemed to consider himself the shepherd of a new Island (see Appendix E).

Amid all the commotion one fact was overlooked. Although it was destroyed by ecumenism, the only truly ecumenical institution on the Island for many decades was the public, non-denominational Prince of Wales College.

A "March of Folly" was underway. Barbara Tuchman's well-known book with that title considers a number of man's worst mistakes.[13] It wonders why, in the field of government, wisdom "which is the exercise of judgment acting on experience, common sense, and available information, is less operative and more frustrated than it should be. . . . Why does intelligent mental process seem so often not to function?" She describes misgovernment as "folly when it is a perverse persistence in a policy demonstrably unworkable or counter productive." These comments fit perfectly the Island's long experience with church politics.

One of Miss Tuchman's best paragraphs is particularly applicable to the Island's politicians and clergy. After quoting Ralph Waldo Emerson's advice – "In analyzing history do not be too profound, for often the causes are quite superficial," she adds her own advice, which is especially needed in my profession. "This is a factor usually overlooked by political scientists who, in discussing the nature of power, always treat it, even when negatively, with immense respect. They fail to see it as sometimes a matter of ordinary men walking into water over their heads, acting unwisely or foolishly or perversely as people in ordinary circumstances frequently do. The trappings and impact of power deceive us, endowing the possessors with a quality larger than life."[14]

This attitude to power mesmerizes observers. Prime Minister Trudeau described being "in bed with an elephant" when dealing with the United States. In Charlottetown the action was "being in bed with" the whole Catholic establishment. It was impossible for Prince of Wales to deal with St. Dunstan's, indeed carry on its own relations with the government, without the Bishop or some of his colleagues getting in the way. His diocese *was* St. Dunstan's. It was perfectly logical, therefore, that E.F. Sheffield, chairman of the local commission on post-secondary education, described the final act as "the merging of St. Dunstan's Basilica and Prince of Wales College."[15] Indeed, most non-Island authorities and observers looked upon the issue in the same way. Prince of Wales' competition was never St. Dunstan's University – it was always the St. Dunstan's diocese.

This type of obstruction was described in a well-known Canadian study of ten new universities of various kinds, edited by Murray Ross, called *New Universities in the Modern World*.[16] Suggested as a "most serious problem" is "the frequently reported resentment of those in established universities at the publicity and status given to the new universities . . . the suspicions, jealousies, and often hostilities of those in older universities do not easily disappear." This resentment is to be expected by most new universities, but it increases inevitably and is harder to combat if church politicians promote it. Indeed the study continued with an opinion directly opposed to one being touted on the Island by the church and the unionists. "A new university given the opportunities that exist in the 1960s has an obligation not just to repeat what is being offered elsewhere but rather to strike out on lines of its own."

But Bishop MacEachern sent a directive to his priests throughout the province: "In the interests of the young people of the province, as well as those who wish to further their own education as adults, St. Dunstan's must be the foundation on which the structure of higher education and adult education for the future is built." Given the circumstances of higher education and church politics on the Island and the superior standard of Prince of Wales, this was an effrontery, defined by the Oxford dictionary as "shameless audacity." (For more details see in Appendix E.)

A good example of how Prince of Wales had "to strike out on its own" and literally fight against the church for "the interests of the young people of the province" was the building of Montgomery Hall, the women's residence. For many decades the Women's Institutes and other organizations had been petitioning the government for a residence, but they were stalled by Catholic representatives in the cabinet, even though the Carnegie Corporation had offered to pay for it in 1930. In 1959 we collected enough money from federal grants and the Department of Public Works with the approval of the Board of Governors and the majority of the cabinet. There was a row in the government and heavy pressure from its Catholic members which we stopped by securing the consent of Governor-General Georges Vanier to lay the cornerstone unusually early, and thus turn the project into a *fait accompli*. We insisted that all the arrangements would be handled, not by Public Works itself, which would be expensive, but by a building committee of three individuals acting alone – the Deputy Minister of Public Works, Gordon White (a valued friend of the College), the architect, and me. We secured the quiet consent from some

of our more understanding authorities to ignore the governing party's patronage list. That was something new for the Island; it worked admirably and was
done with business efficiency, resulting in a splendid building.

The period 1962 to 1968 was decisive for the university question and it
brought forth the worst of church politics. Two reports held views of one side
and the other. One was the "Report of a Citizens' Committee to Study the
Feasibility of Prince of Wales College Becoming a Degree Granting Institution." It was organized in July 1962 under the chairmanship of Dr. Paul
Cudmore, with a fair balance of opinions. The second document was a letter
from Bishop MacEachern to his diocesan clergy dated December 12, 1966.
The Citizens' Committee had many meetings and it consulted widely. It
reported unanimously that it was "entirely feasible from educational, administrative, and financial viewpoints to proceed immediately with the proposal
to elevate Prince of Wales," and it gave reasons. This view, included in
Appendix A, was later supported by a royal commission. On the other hand,
the Bishop's letter was not an appraisal, but a widely distributed ultimatum
undermining Prince of Wales and giving St. Dunstan's an aura it had never
enjoyed. The letter let the Island know that the Bishop's direction was the only
way for the province to go.

It is an old strategy of opponents of democracy to launch appeals against
democratically determined opinions and decisions. When the report of the
Citizens' Committee did not please the church or the unionists, another
committee appeared, called a "study group." Citizens' Committee members
who had supported Prince of Wales were not included; five known for their
readiness to change their minds were. There was no balance of opinions; St.
Dunstan's priests were there, but no faculty from Prince of Wales. What they
called "religion" was displayed extravagantly. It was therefore inevitable that
they should propose a compulsory union of colleges entirely along the lines
of the Catholic demands and opposed to the findings of both the Citizens'
Committee and the provincial Royal Commission on Higher Education. What
they said was bad enough, as Appendix C indicates, but it was a mere
collection of pious platitudes in view of what they ignored completely – the
furious row in the government caucus that was going on behind the scenes
and negated everything the "study group" said. Yet their opinion was extraor-
dinarily naïve: "Frank admission, open acceptance, and free expression of
religious differences can create that situation which makes possible a single
University of P.E.I." This, in a province where expression of religious opinion
has been well nigh impossible, and from a group that showed no capacity to
suggest changes for the better! The only reason their report should receive
attention at all is that it illustrates the dangers of church politics, as well as the

character of men who would preach a policy while ignoring opposing views and the recommendations of the Citizens' Committee, the Royal Commission and the provincial Legislature which had supported Prince of Wales.

The study group's report was so bad, so opposed to any normal approach to education or religion, and so in contrast to what was going on, that I asked for a legal opinion from John P. Nicholson, a prominent lawyer and Baptist Church layman, a member of the Citizens' Committee, and a future Chief Justice of the province.

The report, he wrote, "has as its purpose the frustration of our attempts to make Prince of Wales College a university. It would seem that [the] College must be down-graded to St. Dunstan's standards before we are given an opportunity to begin." "[The document is] unreasonable and impossible if the report of the Royal Commission on Education is to be implemented." One paragraph "has the appearance of something which might have been drafted by a medieval Roman Catholic scholar. The whole tenor of [it] is a 'sop' to unsuspecting Protestants and is as great a trap as I have ever seen laid for an unaware victim. I am prepared to [be] someone who will speak out against an effort by the Roman Catholic Church to control the education system of this province. The rightful place of religion in my opinion is not in a public institution of higher education . . . . You will notice that the proposal asks 'all men of good will' to join with them, the implication, of course, being that anyone who will not join with them is not a man of good will. Propositions such as this can be found in the writings of most 'Jesuits' that I have read. It surprises me that such a philosophy is effective in this day and age."[17]

Hard criticism of the "study group" came from a St. Dunstan's professor: "Not only do I consider your basic assumptions false," wrote Patrick J. MacInnis in an open letter to the group through the press on March 17, 1965, "but I energetically reject the tone and spirit which vitiates your published and oral pronouncements. A spirit which augurs ill for a fruitful solution of this complex problem under your pressures, guidance, or inspiration." He called their spirit "ozymandianism . . . an illusion of mind indulged in by one who deludes himself into thinking that his opinion has but to be expressed in order that it command universal acceptance."

There are two striking facts about this situation. As we have seen, the treatment of Prince of Wales was grossly unfair. It was Bishop Henry O'Leary himself in 1917 who handled the passage of the St. Dunstan's charter under the protection of his Catholic laymen in government. There were no legislative or public discussions, royal commission, citizens' committees, study groups, position papers, or reports for all to see. The public knew nothing. But the Prince of Wales project had all of these, and the church was able to dominate and overcome them. A Catholic may say a private college's elevation was not the public's business. It was, when the private college's authorities divided the Island youth in two, invaded the public college's prerogatives, and asked for public funds for itself while deliberately preventing Prince of Wales from getting public and private funds.

The second striking fact, of which we will see evidence later, is obvious from the names and backgrounds of the participants. Catholic authorities picked the non-Catholic members of the committees, as well as the Catholic ones, and they did it by both direct choice and veto. It is a shrewd procedure which I have watched many times. The result, for the most part, was bright Catholic members of known devotion, and either unstable, uninformed, "red neck" Protestants, or the "nice guy" types – a situation prevented only if a watchful Protestant cabinet minister or another appointer kept an eye on proceedings and introduced alternative nominations. Anyone who knew what was going on in those years could only be appalled at the names of some of the clerics and laity involved in the study group. They were local editions of Jane Austen's Mr. Collins in *Pride and Prejudice,* and Oscar Wilde's Canon Chasuble in *The Importance of Being Ernest.* The clerics appeared to plan their own behavior to fit Keith Spicer's description (pp. 64-65) Unfortunately, it did not take long for those with tight halos to support St. Dunstan's as a group of holy crusaders and to be pressured into regarding Prince of Wales as an assembly of the "godless." (Appendix C illustrates this unfortunate view, and Appendix E confirms the results.)

The situation soon provided a warning of things to come. We had been planning to appoint a chaplain at Prince of Wales and had a first class person in mind. But I had a surprise visit by a member of the "study group," the then Rector of St. Paul's, Charlottetown. He announced that he was the new chaplain of the College and was ready to start forthwith. I replied that we knew nothing about such an appointment, but he persisted unpleasantly and de-parted. I then called his bishop in Halifax whom I knew well, and told him what had happened. It was, he said, the first he had heard of such a thing, and the rector had no authority from anyone. "And you can tell him I said so! Call me again if he bothers you." I telephoned the rector and gave him the message.

There were similar stories about the other "good willers." There were no fewer than seven doctors with the same naïveté and manipulable actions so badly displayed by their confreres in Saskatchewan's famous medicare de-bate. The other fifteen members, including seven priests and ministers and eight lay worthies, had no discernible knowledge of how colleges and univer-sities were organized and run or how appointments to them were made. It was no wonder that the provincial Presbytery of the United Church of Canada informed me that it disassociated itself from the two United Church ministers in the study group, and stood by its own resolution supporting degree-granting status for Prince of Wales. The letter, dated February 25, 1965, is included as Appendix D. One must wonder why the two ministers did not immediately resign from the study group upon this action by their church. One may be sure what would happen if any of the Catholic members had been so disowned by their church. Five members of the group reinforced suspicion about themselves by first agreeing to the unanimous recommendations of the Citizens' Committee, and then supporting the views of the study group which recommended the opposite.

The declarations and actions of this crisis had all the attributes of a game. Unfortunately the Protestant goodwillers did not understand the difference between religion and church politics. Nor did they realize the obvious – that they played the game with the uninformed enthusiasms of the moment, while the Catholic priests and laymen played with continuing tactics tried over the centuries.

One may go beyond the issues and tactics and wonder at the lack of simple Christian concern and kindness from these clergy and laymen about the certainty that 36 or so excellent Prince of Wales faculty members would be forced to give up their jobs, that faculty members had not been asked for opinions to balance church views, and that whatever the goodwillers did would have to end in the destruction of Prince of Wales.

My colleagues and I naturally found it hard to accept the irresponsible meddling of the clerical and lay-game players. I know what they would say in reply. But I am sure that the views of one of the best known politician-clergymen in Canada were nearer ours than those of the goodwillers. "I have always been strongly opposed," wrote Rev. T.C. Douglas, provincial premier of Saskatchewan and federal M.P., "to using religion as a gimmick for gaining political support. . . . We discovered, as one always does in a progressive party, that not only is patriotism the last refuge of the scoundrel, so is religion."[18] Indeed, education in Prince Edward Island not only used religion as a gimmick, but also showed how church politicians who dabble with power in the name of God often try to play Him. That was the real sacrilege.

Church strategy was illustrated in the selection process of the Royal Commission on Higher Education. It was not established to look into the subject of union – every aspect of it had already been examined – but to stop an act of the Legislature elevating Prince of Wales to a university by putting off its proclamation until a commission had reported. It was merely what legislators call a "hoist." What happened in the Cabinet, party caucus, and

Legislature to set up the Commission was not a debate among "men of good will," but a blitzkrieg in March 1964.

The blitzkrieg began with an offensive by Provincial Treasurer Alben Farmer, a son-in-law of Dr. W.J.P. Macmillan. The House opened with endless politicking – the kind of thing A.E. Arsenault prevented at Catholic request when the St. Dunstan's act was being processed. All Protestant members were visited by friends of Prince of Wales while Farmer waged a needling campaign on Premier Shaw and Education Minister L.G. Dewar; meanwhile Farmer's Catholic colleagues visited everybody. The Minister himself recorded a glaring and tragic precedent in public education which he should have opposed and prevented. In addition to being Provincial Treasurer, Farmer was, wrote Dewar, "the chief spokesman for S.D.U. in the government" and "also an ex-officio member of the Board of Trustees of Prince of Wales College."[19] With that unfair arrangement, and because Prince of Wales had no "spokesman" at all in the government, the College's chances were dim. That Shaw and Dewar tolerated it was a fit cause for astonishment.

The government caucus on the College bill was a long, bitter affair. Farmer's tactic was a tantrum on every provision of the bill, and on any government financial responsibility for the College – even though it was government-owned and he was a member of its Board! Dr. Dewar wrote that "most R.C.s I feel are reconciled to the P.W.C. elevation but Farmer apparently threatened to resign or cross the floor of the House."[20] After a vicious fight the bill went through caucus and got first and second readings in the House. Then a respected Catholic minister, Henry Wedge, moved an amendment providing that the act would come into force upon proclamation following receipt and consideration of a report of a royal commission on higher education. March 19, 1964 was a dreadful night in the House. An ultimatum was delivered to Premier Shaw threatening him with the famous old tactic, a religious split in his party.

Non-Catholic members had asked Shaw to call Farmer's bluff since the Catholic position was not defensible in public. I reminded them of how Premier Walter Jones got his divorce and liquor control bills through under worse circumstances – by standing firm. But Shaw would not take the chance, and he broke down and ordered support for the amendment. To everyone's surprise George Dewar, who had introduced this government bill, opposed the amendment at first and then, in spite of the important principle involved and Farmer's tactics, voted for the whole bill as amended. As other members described it, the struggle was over when Shaw and Dewar gave up while Farmer was allowed to ride three horses at once in an astonishing conflict of interest. If either Premier or Minister had stood up to their rebellious Treasurer and been firm, as firm in their strong case as Farmer was in his weak one, Prince of Wales would have been saved.

But the Legislature knew that organized tragedy had once more overcome its prerogatives in favor of church political control, with no trace of good will or religion. "I wish to God," lamented Chairman Robert Grindlay of the House's Education Committee to me, "that I wasn't in politics after what went on last week." And Provincial Secretary David Stewart told me that things had been said in caucus that were so bad they would be remembered by those present for the rest of their lives.[21]

Catholic control over the appointment of the members of the Royal Commission soon appeared. The first three persons agreed upon and contacted were Dr. J.S. Bonnell, Dr. J.A. MacMillan, and Mr. Justice Walter E. Darby. MacMillan, an able and respected physician, was supported in Cabinet by its Catholic members and there was no disagreement. Justice Darby, an experienced legislator and equally respected, was an alumnus of Prince of Wales. The Chairman, Dr. Bonnell, was a retired minister in New York City who was a native Islander. A talented and imposing preacher, his skills were of the social kind. And he was an active symbol not known for taking strong stands. St. Dunstan's had given him an honorary degree the year before, in 1963, as, said the *Guardian*, "the first Protestant to be so honored in the 109-year history of the Roman Catholic University."[22] He also received a medal from the Pope "for ecumenical services" in 1966. The impact of these timely distinctions was not lost on observers.

Yet even this line-up was evidently not satisfactory to Catholic members of the Cabinet. Darby might have some thoughts friendly to Prince of Wales, and he could dominate Bonnell just as MacMillan could. So a quarrel was organized in Cabinet after the appointees had agreed to serve. About six weeks after agreeing to act, Justice Darby wrote me, "I was visited by Dr. Dewar, who after considerable hesitation and apparent embarrassment informed me that my appointment had been opposed by certain religious elements in the Cabinet and that he had been compelled to withdraw his proposal as to my inclusion on the Commission."[23] Dewar himself records that Darby was rejected "mostly because of religious connotations."[24] There was no question of rejecting Darby because he was a judge. At the time, Judge Sylvere DesRoches had been chairman of the Royal Commission on Electoral Reform; and Justice C. St. Clair Trainor had chaired a commission of enquiry into the Georgetown shipbuilding and food processing scandals. Nevertheless the government gave in again when both Premier and Minister did not stand firm. The question lingers – what chance would any non-Catholic minister have if he tried to change a prominent Catholic nominee to a royal commission who had already accepted?

The compromise replacement for Darby was Dr. Norman MacKenzie, an elderly retired president of the University of British Columbia who, as we shall note later, was completely satisfactory to the Catholic cabinet ministers, and was susceptible to control by Catholics in Halifax and Charlottetown. "He was," wrote Dewar, "appointed with some reservations."[25]

Thus encouraged by another surrender, Alben Farmer tried again for the federal grants to Prince of Wales, an attempt with a touch of the Marx Brothers. As Provincial Treasurer, he transferred $160 000 in College funds from the College bank account to general revenue, without consulting anyone at the College. The bank phoned me in bewilderment, and I advised Education Minister Dewar that I would keep the next federal cheque in my desk until it was decided what to do with Farmer. Dewar advised Farmer, instead of giving him a piece of his mind for the impertinence. A few days later I received a bill from Farmer for the interest! Upon being informed, Dewar and Premier Shaw seemed to be petrified of Farmer and fearful of the threatened cabinet split. The obvious and normal remedy for such a difficulty was a cabinet shuffle, with Farmer and Dewar assigned to other portfolios. No-one could have objected. But assault and fear continued. Whereupon I made it clear to the Premier that if our money was spent by anyone else but our Board, or I was legally assailed by Farmer, I would resign and explain all that had happened to the Royal Commission and the Legislature. We got our money back.

Meanwhile the Royal Commission was sitting. It paid no attention to the vicious campaign in the caucus during which the goodwillers were crying hallelujahs out front. Nevertheless, despite all the manoeuvering, it recommended Prince of Wales' cause and emphasized that any subsequent arrangements must be free of any coercion. The details, as noted in Appendix C, were clear enough, but the church politicians continued their assaults.

A commonplace cliché heard at this time was that "politics is the art of the possible" as an excuse for obvious governmental weakness. Politics is no such thing, because many politicians are limited in their knowledge of what is possible and in their strength to pursue it. Successful politics results from leadership, because in much state business leadership is the art of the impossible. Indeed, most great attainments and handling of difficulties started out as "impossible," and impossibility is often an obstacle only because certain people create it.

In addition to the row in the government, two other Catholic tactics raised trouble. One was emphasis on two church categories: 1, us, and 2, everyone else. This dangerous tactical designation is seen nationally when "French Canada" is considered a category and everybody else is "English Canada" or "the rest of Canada." The other tactic states that "for us to get along, the only way is for you to give in to our demands."

The divisive results of these tactics are good enough reasons for separating church and state, to help the work of both and sustain religion itself. But they were allowed to hold the Island back in every aspect of its development and community life.

We should balance the gloom with a representative quartet of the many expressions of support for Prince of Wales at the time. The Secretary of the Women's Institutes wrote me that "we don't hear a dissident voice on the progress of the College." The Dean of Science at the University of Waterloo wrote that "It is refreshing to see evidence of at least one effort to maintain the coherence of university education." And Dr. William Swinton, Centennial Professor at the University of Toronto, who gave guest lectures at Prince of Wales, was enthusiastic about the place. "Everything," he told the *Patriot* and the *Globe and Mail*, "that the academic world looks for is going to be right here in Charlottetown in a wonderful location and as a result you are attracting some of the brightest minds in North America and will attract many more. When these men get together on the faculty some brilliant ideas will result and I foresee the day when your city will be recognized as the 'Iona' of the new world. It will be a wonderful experience and challenge to teach in these surroundings."[26]

In view of all these commotions it was remarkable for me to have a letter from the then ex-Premier Shaw, dated March 17, 1967: "I was amazed," he wrote, "at the progress made in the early Sixties when we conferred together on the proposal of establishing P.W.C. as a university. I am proud indeed to have been associated with this important development!" Exclamation point mine!

Chapter Eight

THE GOING DOWN OF THE SUN

The national aspects of church politics are illustrated by comparing the Ontario separate school question and Prince Edward Island's college issue. As noted earlier, Premier Davis promised to meet demands of the Cardinal Archbishop, on his own, without the consent of Cabinet or Legislature. When the Premier's colleagues expressed doubts he passed them to the Cardinal who held him to the promise as a matter of "honor." On the Island, official promises to elevate Prince of Wales were made – not just by informal conversation this time – but by approval and action of the Board of Governors, Citizens' Committee, Royal Commission, Cabinet, and Legislature. But honor was ignored by the church, even after the promises were implemented and Prince of Wales became a university and functioned very well as such for three years. The Island's Bishop Malcolm MacEachern rejected the obligation of the authorities to stand by their promises and duty, even their own legislation, and literally forced them to renege.

Questions are obvious. Where were democracy, religion, and "men of good will" in this putsch? Where was honor? And to defend honor, where was courage? The replies were provided by clerical action – that church politics has shown itself to be, not a matter of honor, but what the episcopate can get away with; and that in public policy one denomination in Canada has in practice snatched precedence from the state itself. How they got away with it is indicated by contemporary literature on collaboration and resistance in which people's gullibility plays a large part.[1] On the Island a handful of Protestant laymen and clergy did everything possible to apply this description to themselves.

The Prince of Wales College Act, 1964, was proclaimed by the Lieutenant-Governor-in-Council on June 1, 1965, and the College became a university in accordance with the Royal Commission's recommendation to that effect. Following the first meeting of the Board of Governors on June 29, the College applied for admission to the Association of Universities and Colleges of Canada. The Association sent a committee of university educators to visit the College and examine its facilities and plans. Upon the recommendations of this committee and of the national executive, the Association admitted Prince of Wales and five other new universities to membership.

Meanwhile preparatory work had been done; a timetable for the transition was being followed; the new curriculum was ready; new faculty were added and a search for additional ones was in progress. And the cooperation and advice of other universities were available and welcome. Our plans seemed to provide what was needed and suitable for the Island and the Maritime environment. But it was hard for many people to understand the demands of quality – to recognize that universities, like other institutions, are good, mediocre, and bad – and that courses, professors, and degrees vary widely in quality within them.

Fortunately Prince of Wales had enjoyed a high rating throughout Canada and a reputation for quality that never became elitist. Preparations were designed to continue this happy situation. And for good reason. This was a time of competition and industrial and cultural challenge, and the Island desperately needed the educational resources with standards to meet the demands and give students the preparation for life that they deserved.

Statistics indicated the need in 1965. Enrollment in the two existing university years had multiplied almost five times in the previous two years. Prince of Wales had in those two years alone more students than there were in all four years of St. Anne's, King's, and St. Thomas, almost as many as there were in Mt. St. Vincent and Nova Scotia Technical, and proportionately more than several other Maritime universities. On the local scene, Prince of Wales had more university students in two years than St. Dunstan's had in all four years, five years earlier. To project, Prince of Wales in two years would have more students than Acadia, Mt. Allison and St. Francis Xavier had a short time previously. The Association of Atlantic Universities estimated that 1 000 students were denied admission to Atlantic provinces universities because of overcrowding in 1965-6; the figure was estimated as 8 000 for 1970. All these figures were in my annual report to the board and the government for 1964-5 and were well known at the time.

We started in 1965 with planning the freshman year to meet the changes, and in 1966 with the sophomore year. The first junior year was added in 1967, and the first senior year in 1968. The first degrees were awarded in 1969. All the courses added were new and at the advanced levels required; we carefully avoided the old Maritime practice of some universities of adding more existing elementary work to fill out the program. And we added ideas from people who knew industry and employment and encouraged fresh academic approaches to them.

To celebrate its new status and to contribute to the 1967 centennial program, Prince of Wales held a Commemorative Centennial Convocation on September 29. Representatives of universities from coast to coast attended and honorary degrees were presented to a number of distinguished Canadians headed by Prime Minister L.B. Pearson. Three hundred guests sat down to a memorable dinner, after which a thousand guests, alumni, and friends danced at a gala Convocation Ball in the Confederation Centre of the Arts. Another thousand students celebrated at a Student Ball in the College auditorium, with the special guests circulating at both events.

Things at Prince of Wales were going much too well for her critics, and all signs pointed to the college's splendid future. But the way was opening up for another assault, an appeal against the decisions of democracy. A general election was coming in 1966, with a probability of defeating the Conservatives for their industrial mistakes in Georgetown. The usual clerical and lay goodwillers were rounded up again in crusade formation; and a new group joined them that anticipated favors and advancement from a new government and would not hesitate to cultivate the Catholic vote. Every temptation was put in their way and preferment was promised to those whose integrity was known to be for sale, just like it was when Father Joseph combined spiritual weapons with "more mundane forms of persuasion," including "gifts . . . pensions, honors, positions in the administration." Over many months I watched this wooing of the untrustworthy and heard many stories of shady deals involving people whose interest was only in themselves. "There's no explaining them," said Harry Truman; "Birds like that are just part of the dirt that comes up when we're in for a run of hysteria in this country."[2]

The election took place on May 30, 1966 and resulted in a tie, with 15 members returned for each side in the 32-seat House. The First Kings contest had been deferred on the death of a candidate. The two seats left in the dual constituency were therefore crucial, and the fight was on with every weapon – promises, liquor, road machines, bribery, patronage, money. No holds were barred. "If it moves pension it," said a popular joke, "if it doesn't, pave it." Church interests were well promoted, not just on the college question, but also on securing a senatorship for the retiring Catholic federal member of Parliament. Prime Minister Pearson told me at the convocation dinner that he had never received as many letters from priests and laymen as he did for that appointment. He also agreed that a union of the colleges had all the attraction of a coalition between him and Mr. Diefenbaker.

The two seats went Liberal, the Shaw government resigned on July 28, and a new administration took over with Alexander B. Campbell as Premier.

Canada's oldest premier, 78, was replaced by the youngest, 32. Charlottetown's Bishop knew exactly how to proceed from there.

The dust had hardly settled after the election when intense activity stirred among the Catholic supporters of a college union and the goodwillers who still cruised over the shoals like pilot fish with sharks. The time was now ripe for their final siege, because the new inexperienced government was wide open to pressure and vulnerable with its one-seat majority following the selection of the Speaker. Ecumenism, not yet repudiated by the Pope, was laid on, indeed shovelled on, by its Island disciples, thus turning the assault into a crusade. But this was just the rifle chatter. The Big Gun was rolled out to fire an episcopal bomb, Bishop Malcolm MacEachern's letter to his priests dated December 12, 1966. It is discussed in Appendix E.

As the letter indicates, the basic flaw was its main and pretentious attraction. He offered "a first move toward a partnership with Protestants of good will – a university of a Christian orientation though not related to any particular denomination." This was the ecumenical Trojan Horse again, but this time it was even less attractive because there had been no apparent good will or Christianity in union developments up to now, and there was obviously little chance of "orientation" not being "related to any particular denomination." The Bishop wrote of "the hard and unreasonable line taken by P.W.C.!" He wanted action now "lest Dr. MacKinnon personally or through the P.W.C. Board made another announcement committing themselves in the course they have unilaterally chartered." Were we not given the right to do just that by the Legislature and the Royal Commission backed by the Citizens' Committee? Had we not proceeded according to all the recognized principles of higher education, while the Bishop and his associates broke them all and made a parody of democracy, parliamentary government and, yes, of religion? And had not all Catholic politics in college education over the decades been entirely unilateral with no cooperation offered to anyone, only dominance and, for Prince of Wales, only meddling and opposition? Having disposed of us, he then gave his priests cheerful news of the "excellent relationship which the President-Rector of S.D.U. established with the Premier last month." Of course the Rector did; he had the new Premier exactly where he wanted him, and his Bishop was in charge.

Indeed, the Bishop, and only the Bishop, now had the future in his hands, and he was able to take an arbitrary approach in announcing the future policy. Although he offered a "partnership with Protestants of good will," and established the "relationship" with the Premier, he nailed his own plan to the masthead: "St. Dunstan's must be the foundation on which the structure of higher education and adult education for the future is built." This was the same kind of arbitrary statement Pope John Paul used to end ecumenism, but neither the Island ecumenists nor the government understood its significance. The Bishop's sentence actually was the "hard and unreasonable line," the "unilateral" action, and it should have ended the matter there and then, because it was the main obstacle to any voluntary union and it flew in the face of all constitutional authority. It was not for the Bishop to decide, but he did decide, and no-one said him "nay."

The Bishop's letter demolished, for example, the report of the government's own Royal Commission. The Commission recommended a federation "if it should be found desirable and feasible," and "only as it is the expression of will and desire of all parties to the union and is free from any element of coercion." It also recommended that the Prince of Wales Board proceed immediately to establish the four-year program, and that "it is very important that the government provide the necessary funds." Appendix B presents the highlights. It is likely that the row in the Legislature which established its authority prompted the Commission to add the qualifications to its recommendations in order to protect Prince of Wales from further onslaughts, but to no avail. Although the Bishop's cohorts in effect set up the Commission and selected its members to suit themselves, they immediately started appeals from it, and the government gave in. Similarly the government ignored the unanimous report of the Citizens' Committee which was allowed to fade into the background while the clerical fantasies of the study group became propaganda for the Bishop's cause.

What did the boards of governors say? St. Dunstan's Board met soon after the Bishop's letter appeared and of course it was approved. What else could they do? He was their Bishop and Chancellor. Prince of Wales' Board resolved to continue its plans and policies. It offered cooperation with St. Dunstan's when necessary. And the two Boards met for a cordial, if formal discussion.

An important comment appeared in the statement of the P.W.C. Board's chairman. "We had two eminent authorities visit us and they gave us frank opinions . . . two in particular impressed us . . . it is more costly to run a combination of two than two separate institutions. . . . The internal politics of a combination is frustrating, expensive and inefficient. . . . It is extremely difficult to get things done, and the result is often compromise which pleases no one and frustrates everyone with a resulting mediocrity which produces second or third rate education."[3]

"Here on the Island," I said at the same meeting, "we have always had the two institutions and dual educational facilities have been accepted in our school system. The adding of two extra years at Prince of Wales doesn't alter any existing situation; nor does it affect St. Dunstan's in the slightest because virtually all P.W.C. sophomore graduates went to the mainland. There has never been any competition for students between the two colleges and there is not likely to be any in the future. Our full time student enrollment has doubled twice in the past four years and our part-time student enrollment has quadrupled in one year."

What did the Bishop say to that? No doubt he uttered an episcopal snort as he penned these lines to his priests: "Exchange of inane pleasantries, greetings, etc., is only cooperation with a lollypop tradition and flavour. . . . It is felt that the appointment of a joint committee of the two boards is a meaningless gesture – mere window dressing . . . a sort of a Pearl Harbor reenactment." Translated this means "so much for cooperation, now I'll take over – again."

We should ask what St. Dunstan's could have done. The answer is nothing; it had no power or discretion of its own and displayed no tradition of academic principles generally associated with universities. And Prince of Wales? Being a public university now, it could not fail its duty by submitting itself to the will of the Bishop. And what could the Bishop have done? The answer was obvious; he could have got out of the way. As long as he and his team hovered over everything and burrowed under anything, it was not possible to reach a sensible and effective conclusion. He must have his way, and the government had allowed itself to be put in a position to give it to him.

What could the government have done? And what could the Premier have said? And how could he have avoided negative reaction? The answer was simple and obvious – tell the truth, and assert the principles of public ownership which it was the government's duty to protect (see pp. 63-64). A statement after attaining office, or an announcement in the Legislature, could thus have presented the facts: "The government of Prince Edward Island is responsible, on behalf of the Legislature and people, for the publicly owned institutions in this province, of which Prince of Wales College has had a distinguished history since 1834. The previous government has already taken and completed the necessary steps for the College's contemporary development. It was supported by a freely organized Citizens' Committee, the Royal Commission on Higher Education, numerous citizens and consultants, and the Legislative Assembly which, after full debate, passed the Prince of Wales College Act. The College's Board of Governors and Faculty have been well along in their work for three years, and professional recognition is complete. If there are to be associations between two institutions, it is up to them to make the decision and arrange the details. As the Royal Commission said in its report, there must be no coercion."

"Accordingly, why should this government now cancel the decision of the last one, flout all the recommendations and wishes of the Legislature, and destroy its own university that has served our people well? Should anyone disapprove, we tell them that the House and Government are required to run this province under due process of law, and have acted democratically after more than enough consideration of facts and opinions. They have no intention of neglecting this duty, and no reason has been put forward why they should change existing policy just because of a narrowly won election. And they hope the future will bring the Island's university authorities, faculties and students every success." If this statement had been made it would have been very difficult to refute in public. But the Premier passed by on the other side.

As always in these issues, cost was important. But it was mentioned only when the public college needed something, and the theme then was "little Prince Edward Island can't afford it." But in any church question, such as separate schools and university union, cost is readily accepted and justified no matter how high it turns out to be. "We cannot afford two colleges" was not said when St. Dunstan's opened or in later years, as the church's approach was "you'd better afford it," or "it is God's will." The tune changed when the federal grants to universities appeared, especially when they were siphoned through provincial governments. And it changed again when Prince of Wales developed as it should. Then the cry against the cost arose. But it was shushed as all the eight Maritime Catholic colleges blossomed forth at public expense with no questions asked.

As for what the Island could afford, we at Prince of Wales and most of our consultants estimated it would cost much more to run the two colleges together than separately, and that assessment proved correct. We also predicted a costly financial situation in the use of federal educational funds by the provincial government, which itself contributed little or nothing.[4]

But ideas of cost were not good bases for argument by either church or government in view of their rejection of Sir William Macdonald's generous funds that would have provided all the university facilities the Island would need and much economic enterprise as well. Land, buildings, funds, endowments, academic facilities and services, teaching staff, research, cooperation with government, business, industry, and the agricultural college for the Maritimes – all were in the magnificent plan of which Prince of Wales was to have been the instrument. The rejection has already been a tragic lost opportunity for 88 years, and it was, and continues to be, an ongoing liability. The cost amounts to hundreds of millions of dollars, putting the Island's carelessness among the most expensive follies in higher education in Canada, and leaving the province in its continuing doldrums of minimal and marginal enterprise.

This situation, as described so far, was the church backdrop for the final act of the university drama. Unfortunately the economic backdrop was suit-able for tragedy and comedy playing together simultaneously on one small stage with inexperienced casts. Because of it, Island public affairs were unstable in the 1960s, and more easily meddled with than ever. The govern-ment had two large and excellent economic opportunities which it seemed unable to comprehend or carry out – a Georgetown industrial project and a provincial development plan. The two administrations of the decade were over their heads in unfamiliar business, and the public soon wondered what would happen next and what they would get for the vast amounts the Shaw and Campbell governments were spending. It was Prince of Wales' misfortune that its business got mixed up with general governmental failure on the Island in the 1960s.

The economic scandals involved fish processing and shipbuilding projects in Georgetown, sponsored by the Conservatives, and an "Island development plan" presented by the Liberals.[5] These scandals and church politics in the college issue became a high-priced three-ring circus, with Walter Shaw, Bishop MacEachern, and Alex Campbell as ring masters, and the Bishop as master of ceremonies above the centre ring.

The idea of a fish plant and shipbuilding business in Georgetown was originally sensible and practical. There was a demand for the projects, and prospects were good at the time for meeting expenses and making profits. Those who run such enterprises should know what they are doing, but politicians with no knowledge or experience in industry were trying to direct fish processing and shipbuilding. They needed informed advice, but knew neither where to seek it nor how to take it. The Premier, minister in charge, Provincial Treasurer, and the leading administrative officers acted like fat men trying to dance ballet without skill, lessons, or practice. The result was a clumsy, comical, costly failure.

One would think that a lesson would have been learned and assessments kept on file, in case of future efforts of this kind. But this is not the way it worked out. The Liberals took over, and, like many new administrations, they rushed to get a project of their own, a development plan. All the mistakes the Conservatives had made they repeated, with similar results. However the development plan appeared on paper, it was bound to fail without able people to run it. Once again ministers and advisors stumbled around. And some of the advisors were examples of an old Island problem – consulting or hiring staff without avoiding other people's discards. A premier from a neighboring province, for example, related to me with hilarity how he had unloaded on the Island premier a notorious incompetent whom his government had long tried to get rid of. Plans and efforts were frustrated by catering to consumer service rather than the demands of production. "Creating jobs" was a popular tactic, but a short-sighted one without a permanent industrial structure to sustain them. Such a structure did not materialize, millions of dollars disappeared, much of it federal money, and what was left was small in relation to the great expectations.

The Georgetown and development plan failures together indicate a multi-million dollar scandal. Island politicians themselves agreed with this judgment – the Liberals when discussing the Conservative debacle, and the Conservatives when blaming the Liberals for theirs. But the problem was deeper than that. Between them the two governments succeeded only in damaging the provincial economy and government itself. And the money they wasted could have financed at least a half dozen universities.

Island cultural and intellectual enterprises suffer from the same problems as economic ones. But in this instance the approach tends to be negative and restrictive. Censoring or prohibiting uncomfortable ideas and projects that might offend someone, are things one gets used to on the Island and tries to circumvent. They illustrate the "politically correct" movement.

A lively, almost comic affair a few years later was typical. The Confederation Centre of the Arts presented a musical about Elvis Presley, "Are You Lonesome Tonight?" Objections were raised, but the production went on as scheduled and played to appreciative packed houses. At the next annual meeting of the Centre's board directors attended the controversial but excellently produced musical. Next day we learned from one board member that a clergyman had telephoned him to protest Elvis, and to advise that he had told his congregation the previous Sunday that parents should forbid their children from attending the show. What were we going to do about it? Neither the board member nor the clergyman had seen the performance, so the obvious advice to them was to attend before criticizing what they knew nothing about. I suggested the board member tell the cleric to preach another sermon advising the parents to send their teenagers to what was a fine contemporary morality play. They would enjoy it, and most important, they would see the results of drink and drugs properly highlighted as no priest or parent could do.

All this skittishness about politics, economics, and culture confused governments and people when the college issue needed initiative, efficiency, and common sense. Indeed, had Prince of Wales' plan been allowed to continue after its excellent start, new achievements in teaching and research could have helped solve Island problems like Georgetown and the development plan. The faculty had already included experience in these fields, and many of the new members were well trained for this task. And it could all have been much less costly than the college union proved to be, and practically free of cost altogether compared with the futile extravagance of the provincial government's economic fantasies.

Come now! someone may exclaim; how do you know? Is this not wishful thinking? To reply I can justly refer him to the other project going on at the same time – the conception, planning, financing, construction, and managing of the Confederation Centre, the leadership of which came from within Prince of Wales College (pp. 83-85). Often described as a perfectly-managed multi-million dollar large-scale enterprise, it was the only one of the Island's big projects of the 1960s that succeeded. And it gave every promise of the Prince of Wales university project being successful.

It was in the 1960s setting of mayhem that the Bishop directed the final scenes of his campaign, which he himself indicated in his letter. He had succeeded beyond anyone's dreams with Father Helmick's third verb in his church's strategy, and "suppressed." Now, with everyone else thoroughly confused about Island affairs, it was a good time to make the final move.

The Catholic strategy therefore changed from advocating supposed merits of union; there were none anyway – and Prince of Wales' progress and public acceptance were too substantial. Separate, federated, or united universities could not be tolerated by the Bishop and he indicated that in his letter. The new weapon was therefore the big stick, hitherto held in obvious reserve – the threat of a thundering "religious" row. Either a union was forced or the faithful would be marshalled on the hustings and in door-to-door campaigns and public declarations against Prince of Wales. This was the same ultimatum used in all separate school rows in Canada, and, as we noted, it appeared again in the Premier/Cardinal encounter in Ontario (pp. 50-51). Now here was the dreaded crisis on the Islanders' doorstep.

The traditional marshalling of acquiescence proceeded rapidly. As much as the many officials and citizens liked the new three-year-old university status of Prince of Wales and what was happening there, the prospect of a dreaded church confrontation was urged upon them. The subject was not debatable – it was union or else. How comforting the alternative seemed: let's all get together in the spirit of ecumenism. Consultants who had been led to favor the plan had this idea forced upon them without the facts, and they accepted the episcopal threat as the only alternative. Consultants who spoke for Prince of Wales were ignored. How often was "If I had only known" heard later!

Behind the scenes church strategy was being projected beyond anyone's expectations. I talked to so many people about the situation and why it developed as it did; the reply was virtually unanimous. If Prince of Wales and its friends had to deal only with the Bishop and his company they could argue with impunity and consultants would have a reasonable base for their opinions. But a few uninformed non-Catholic clergy and laymen gave an element of alleged Christian unity to the crisis which seemed impossible to combat. And their intensity was such that the Bishop had all the encouragement he needed to go as far as he could as quickly as possible. The chance was there, why not go for the limit – make Prince of Wales a sacrifice to Island "religious interests," promote St. Dunstan's as the Bishop's "foundation for the future," and do it with speed.

This arrangement was the only apparent way to overcome a contradiction in policies – that of separate schools and universities for Catholics, and that of ecumenism and college union. This paradoxical ecumenical separatism could not work as the Bishop proposed in his letter unless Prince of Wales disappeared, and unless the Island's government and Premier were prevented from defending the principles of public ownership from church politics.

These developments were best explained to me later by a respected Catholic who disliked what went on. Once the church set forth the strategy, he said, it was not surprising that the faithful accepted it. What astonished him was how quickly the non-Catholic goodwillers stampeded once again. Indeed, he emphasized his view that Prince of Wales was destroyed by strategic persons who had taken thirty pieces of silver. My friend was right. The last stage of the campaign (the "destroy" one) was embarked on because these people made it possible to an extent that not even the Bishop could have expected, by cutting the ground out from under friends of the College and other interested citizens.

Strategically placed persons were manoeuvred on the educational chessboard. A good example of how the strategies were handled was seen in the figure of Norman MacKenzie, a Nova Scotian known for his addiction to committees. He had voted with the unanimous Island Royal Commission. As Chairman of the Nova Scotia University Grants Commission (U.G.C.), he had failed in his attempts to cut the number of Nova Scotia universities; they increased from ten to thirteen. His handlers were patient and skillful with him and he made no progress. One of these was Msgr. Hugh Somers, executive officer of the Maritime Association of Universities and Colleges and an old associate of Bishop MacEachern at St. Francis Xavier. Somers was a frequent visitor to Charlottetown, introduced around town in support of "one university," a policy directly opposite to that of his own province, and of his own church elsewhere. Another handler was the able and charming President of Mount St. Vincent, Sister Catherine Wallace. They and others encouraged MacKenzie to go to the Island where he could get his wish to tout union, despite the well-known fact, which his biographer Peter Waite records, that he "neither cared for nor understood what a university really was."[6] But he followed Somers to the Island and called on authority and learned of the threatened church disturbances. He was persuaded to support the peaceful alternative, and he advocated it. As he said later, his views went only so far; he was not told the ultimate goal and he was soon pushed aside.[7]

MacKenzie's biography describes a delightful scene of business between MacKenzie and Sister Wallace. The words are applicable to many contacts involved in the college question. Sister Catherine, wrote the author, "instructed her nuns and colleagues never to raise awkward questions at meetings with the U.G.C. . . . 'Leave these gentlemen to me,' she would say. Larry was always susceptible to attractive and intelligent women, especially those who sustained the delicious hypocrisy of concealing what they were after."

At this point the various opposing strategies came together and Prince of Wales supporters could do nothing because the threatened clerical row had by now appeared dangerous to many people. They, and I, felt much like Archbishop Garnsworthy did in the Ontario racket – helpless. A so-called "gentlemen's agreement" seemed to many a safe compromise because they and various authorities never knew that Prince of Wales was to be destroyed and St. Dunstan's continued. They were misled by "those who sustained the delicious hypocrisy of concealing what they were after." Unpleasantness would be avoided. Ecumenism was featured. "Religion" was supposedly honored. Why worry?

The government need not worry. They could take what was made to appear the easiest way, the Catholic way, as the line of least resistance and the "politically correct" solution at the moment. And the Protestants would accept it as inevitable because, thanks to their goodwillers, they had given everything away and were now powerless to do anything.

Accordingly, Premier Campbell made a policy statement on post-secondary education in the Legislature on April 1, 1968. He announced that the government would support "a single public university in Prince Edward Island, a merger between two degree granting institutions of equal size." Then, and in the following months, his government gave the Catholic church everything it wanted and more. It let the Bishop's wishes and St. Dunstan's standards push Prince of Wales and its much higher standards right out of the subsequent politics and into oblivion.

The Premier's statement must have been met with delight at the palace. It could have been composed there, or vetted in the government by one of the Bishop's acolytes. There was not a word, not a suggestion, of the real issues behind the university question – the often sordid history of church politics and the aggressive church policy (which the Bishop had declared in his letter) that was expected to be maintained in the new institution. The Premier's statement included carefully selected quotations and advice from various reports, most of which were largely irrelevant because they did not make allowances for the power of Island church politics, and because none of the authorities' more demanding (perhaps more embarrassing) advice was included in the statement.

An experienced Islander pronounced a suitable verdict on the Premier's statement. He was Millar MacLure, a former faculty member at Prince of Wales and now chairman of an English department at the University of Toronto. "The actions of this Government," he wrote, "seem from the distance, high-handed in the extreme and lacking in any sense of the organic development of universities and importance of their autonomy."[8]

I resigned on April 8, 1968 and it took almost two weeks for the Board of Governors to accept. I was left with no alternative. "Although," I said, "the government was kept completely informed of developments at Prince of Wales and although its approval of our plans was sought and obtained . . . it never advised its own public university that there was a change contemplated, nor did it give the College an opportunity to express any opinions. . . . The question inevitably arises – where does such intervention end? Who can work in a situation which does not inspire confidence in the future?"[9]

From then on I had no further connection with higher education on the Island, and enjoyed a most happy university career in Calgary.

But I had the sad experience of hearing how quickly disillusionment set in after the change. For example, promises had been made or assumed, not on paper, but in the enthusiastic talk of the campaign for union. I heard them all. They were important to many people in making up their minds, but once the government made its announcement they were forgotten. Several subjects were of special importance.

1. The Bishop, it was said, had agreed to sell the St. Dunstan's campus for $1, which seemed reasonable because it was the church that wanted and forced the union and was the only beneficiary. What happened was that a large purchase price was paid, although Prince of Wales campus was available for nothing; it was assumed the money went to the church instead of the new university.

2. The phasing out of priests and nuns was commonly understood and, it was said, two nearby convent buildings would be purchased for the new university. But the clergy stayed and the convents remained next door to cast a powerful image over the campus.

3. If the new university decided, after studying the relative merits of the two campuses, to develop Prince of Wales' one, it could use or dispose of the St. Dunstan's campus as it wished, perhaps for a new agricultural institute. The Bishop's wish was followed although it was the less desirable alternative. Indeed I was told on excellent authority that the Prince of Wales plans were never discussed.

4. The two institutions would disappear, and their enabling legislation would be ended with union, one new university only continuing. What happened was that Prince of Wales disappeared while St. Dunstan's was allowed to remain and act in its own name. It can pop up any time, and neither the government nor the new university will be able to stop it when the circumstances permit.

St. Dunstan's did not wait for those circumstances, and attempted a major take-over too soon and right after the union. It asked the Board of the new university to set up "the St. Dunstan's College programme" in the Faculty of Arts and on one year's notice. St. Dunstan's University "shall have the right to establish and undertake departments and courses in any or all subjects of the University curriculum in which it had departments and courses prior to" the union, in which case "it shall be entitled to appoint and maintain its own administrative and instructional staff. . . . The S.D.U. negotiators asked that the proposals be kept confidential and that they not be discussed in open meetings."[10] The U.P.E.I. President strongly opposed these proposals and the Board unanimously rejected them. No wonder! Such a scheme, followed by opposition to duplication, would enshrine church control by preventing U.P.E.I. from making any such arrangements and appointments and having control over policy and standards.

It is appropriate to cite the U.P.E.I. newspaper on the manoeuvre: "Although this document is classified as confidential we feel it is important people realize what was going on during the amalgamation negotiations in the summer of 1969." The Board and President "should be commended for their unanimous stand against such insane proposals."[11]

This dishonest episode confirmed all the reasons for opposition to the union on the part of Prince of Wales. It also illustrated again how one-sided the approach to union had been, and what could be expected in the future. Furthermore, Prince of Wales was far better prepared with its existing and new staff to set up courses and appoint faculty, and its program had been in successful operation in its years as a university before union was announced.

On hearing of the new "confidential" and "not to be discussed" Catholic plan which was a radical departure from anything proposed earlier, and a bad portent for cooperation in the future, the provincial government could have done the Island a great service by announcing that the as yet un-implemented union would be cancelled immediately and the two universities reinstated. Church politics would have received a needed check. After all the earlier commotion the public, Catholic and Protestant, would understand the cancellation and the Island government would have been honored for a strong democratic stand, and a much needed reform on behalf of religion. Indeed, a return to the two universities might well have had a salutary national effect.

The Island's Catholic manoeuvers on the local scale are obvious on the national one. Quebec's sovereignty and separatist tactics, which are actually Catholic ones, have been presented vigorously in a one-sided campaign (as chapter 2 suggested) with little or no historic or practical justification. That is one tactic. But another, which is alien to all normal ideas of democracy and fair play, is the suggestion that Quebec can say what it likes but "the rest of Canada" must not offend Quebec by expressing opinions and challenging arguments. This was a feature of church politics on the Island. A third tactic is turning the issues into a great public surge by limiting severely what Quebecers hear, even misinforming them – what Saskatchewan's Premier Roy Romanow called a "con job." Mr. Romanow, reported the *Globe and Mail*, "took exception to the notion that political leaders outside Quebec must choose their words about Quebec cautiously."[12]

"Going to Paris," said the Premier about federal Opposition Leader Lucien Bouchard's visit to France in May 1994, "is not inflammatory, but for me to comment on it is inflammatory? No."[13] In Island terms, Bishop MacEachern, W.J.P. MacMillan, and Alben Farmer were inflammatory to excess, protected by the curious mistaken notion that they spoke for religion, and that questioning them would be inflammatory. As for "con jobs," Islanders have had too many.

The danger to Canada as a whole is obvious. There are now many signs of the church political tactics that were used historically to expel the Huguenots, manoeuver the Acadians, and frustrate the Anglican Archbishop of Toronto.

When Lucien Bouchard promised to defend francophone rights he should have been told what the Huguenot and Acadian issues and the Duplessis regime indicated – that any danger to francophones has come from other francophones. There appears to be a repetition of what Gérard Pelletier called "the inevitable collusion between an excessive clericalism and a corrupt regime . . . [in which]the spiritual powers had for a long time exceeded their proper role" (see pp. 41-42). These tactics of church politics transferred to other aspects of life were destructive in the Island's higher education system. Prevention is necessary lest the same tactics in national affairs result in the destruction of Canada.

The question arises whether church politicians are advising officials or rallying the faithful about business vital to the future of Canada, particularly on the constitution, and doing it badly. Some authorities indicate dangerous examples. Don Jamieson, well-known in Newfoundland provincial and federal politics, reported that "the Catholic Archbishop of St. John's (Most Rev. E.P. Roche) advised his flock to oppose Confederation because he feared that exposure to the outside world would tempt them away from the faith and endanger funding for the Catholic School system."[14] A Laval scholar, Esther Delisle, pronounced judgment on Quebec's influential Abbé Lionel Groulx: "An educator and prolific author, he loathed parliamentary democracy and yearned to replace it with a Mussolinian type of authoritarian regime. His vision of a racially pure French Catholic state (within or without Confederation) excluded all others."[15] If authorities follow E. Davie Fulton's opinion, mentioned earlier, "that the prudent solution will always be the Catholic solution," then it is time to discuss evidence.

Prudence has not shown itself in church politics in Prince Edward Island and countless other places. And it is not likely that unquestioned clerical advice on public business can ever be prudent without open and responsible discussion. When church negotiators ask that their proposals "be kept confidential and that they not be discussed in open meetings," they do not express religious or democratic wishes, and certainly not academic ones. It is an intrusive spillover from church politics to public life.

Another spillover is the assault on freedom of speech. Parti Québecois leader Jacques Parizeau revealed much when he warned financial authorities to cease reporting on possible disadvantages of separation or they might invite reprisals. Premier Daniel Johnson was reported as accusing him of "acting like a tin-pot dictator."[16]

Of all aspects of freedom of speech in difficult times, surely the right of citizens to be told both acceptable and controversial aspects of their history should be maintained. These should include hearing why some 300 000 English-speaking Montrealers emigrated from Quebec in the last 20 years. The celebrated film *The Rise and Fall of English Montreal*, a National Film Board special on the CBC was long anticipated. But the *Calgary Herald* reported that "certain others" did not wish the film telecast.[17] The film was shown and it revealed much of what every citizen should know. It is no wonder that Preston Manning observed that Quebec separatists "talk loud and long about democracy and freedom and all of that. . . . But when anybody disagrees with them they're extremely quick to exhibit pretty arbitrary behavior. I don't think that's a good sign. I think democracy could be one of the first casualties in an independent Quebec."[18] Both the Duplessis regime and the Island's college problem indicate how the casualty would result from church politics, not constitutional problems.

Many aspects of Quebec's situation in Canada are accurately discussed by the well-known bi-cultural Quebec writer William Johnson in his valuable *A Canadian Myth.*[19] "The people of Quebec," he wrote in 1994, "have been misled . . . taken down several garden paths [with] much disinformation, so many illusions propagated over so many years." What Quebec needs is "liberation from reactionary anglophobia and the reactionary ethnic state." He notes the unappreciated fact that it was English-speaking Canadians "who had largely brought the economic development of Quebec to one of the highest levels in the world" and then were regarded as "despoilers of the dream of a French Quebec." That this "tribalist vision could gain acceptance . . . is an astonishing phenomenon" explained by the "demonization of les Anglais."

Johnson refers to Abbé Lionel Groulx as having "more influence on the thinking of French Canada than anyone else in the twentieth century." Groulx with his racially pure French Catholic state wanted "to prune" anglophone "foreign growth" from French culture to purify it. As a student in Montreal in Groulx's day I thought this the silliest of all his intellectual and clerical betrayals. He was actually weakening Quebec's culture, in the same way his predecessors weakened Quebec and Canada by pruning the Huguenots. "Pure" culture, like steel without alloy, is hard and brittle rather than hard and strong. I believe this is still true in Quebec, and it is also a weakness of the "Island way of life" and localism in Newfoundland. We should note again that this urge to "purity," as a political strategy that usually leads to authoritarianism, is clerical but not religious, and as such, is sustained by being kept "confidential and not discussed in public." Censorship follows, of course, as illustrated in the well known attempts to stop CBC productions of *The Boys of St. Vincent* and the *Rise and Fall of Old Montreal* from being televised.

A contemporary issue in western Canada also illustrates the imprudence of church politics on a national scale. Dr. Hugo A. Meynell, professor of Religious Studies at the University of Calgary, himself a Catholic, opposed the suggested inclusion of a new St. Mary's College in the public university. "Catholicism," he wrote, in a letter to the *Calgary Herald* of September 20, 1994, "along with other kinds of religious thought, is taught at the university in a fully ecumenical context. . . . Why should one religious community have special educational privileges, beyond those which it already enjoys by law? . . . Have some people so little faith in their faith that they think it cannot flourish in a free market of ideas? . . . Why have another such institution, except perhaps to replace education with indoctrination? . . . What is really at stake is the control of information in the interests of ecclesiastical power – which is precisely what has led to the appalling scandals which now disfigure the Roman Catholic Church in Canada."

In these and other issues I have noted the consistency with which the church has applied the verbs Father Raymond Helmick discussed – *coopt, ruin, suppress,* and *destroy.* The action continued from the persecution and expulsion of the French Protestants in Canada's early days, through many rows and to the destruction of Prince of Wales. One may wonder, therefore, if we have reached the point where too much that is splendid and successful about Canada is still caught up in this deplorable four-verb process.

These views on both sides of Canada's issues, including the policy statements of Abbé Groulx and Bishop MacEachern, need frank uncensored expression and debate in legislatures, the media, scholarship, and public opinion. They have not had this discussion yet, only pussy-footing, defined in Webster as moving "with stealth or caution as a cat does – to avoid committing oneself or making one's position clear." Unfortunately when stealthy pussy-footers meet a cat-fight follows. Canadians and their governments and churches cannot afford the destructive feline activity of church politics that is kept "confidential and not to be discussed in open meetings" by "those who sustained the delicious hypocrisy of concealing what they were after" (see pp. 114-115).

The history of Island church politics indicates more harmful manoeuvers in the future. They will continue to succeed if there are "gentlemen's agreements," confidential and not discussed in the open. The signs are already ominous for public universities. "Maritime Christian College," described by its president as "a full degree-granting institution entitled by the province," will offer "everything from one-year basic Bible training to a five-year bachelor of theology program." This institution purchased the Mount St. Mary's monastery across the road from the U.P.E.I. campus. All of which "makes us a much more visible post-secondary institution."[20] And Bishop MacEachern had served notice that his policy must determine "the structure of higher education" in the province; there is now a St. Dunstan's Board of Governors within U.P.E.I. with its present Bishop as its Chancellor to carry on!

It was a tragic disservice that the inexperienced "goodwillers" did to the Island when they neglected to obtain some clear agreements on paper while they had the chance. Instead of just deciding there should be a union with much "religion" and leaving it at that, they should have tried to get some consensus on the terms, and above all some limitations on church politics, for the sake of academic principles and standards. Then they would have seen first hand what the difficulties would be. Acceptance of something "in principle" is easy, but it is fatal in negotiations if practical realities are not discussed right at the start, along with the principle. Those who leave details left "to be worked out later" win hands down. ("Come into my parlor said the spider to the fly.") If well-prepared clerics with episcopal supervision are involved, "agreement in principle" is too easily claimed as gospel, or "honor" as Cardinal Carter called it. Then only they have final control over the details.

At that stage on the Island, discussion and the advice of consultants were based only on a *fait accompli* with the threat of a "religious" row in the background. There was little the remaining Prince of Wales people could do because, as her former registrar said after staying on only a year, "the dream that died is being buried with indecent haste."[21] Sixteen of the best faculty members left within a few months, to be snapped up by other universities, and about the same number of able new prospective staff decided not to come. No-one resigned until after the last knell had been sounded. The saddest result was the loss to the Island of this outstanding group, the best faculty of academics that had ever been secured for the province.

Many Islanders and outside authorities have since come to regret the union or become ashamed of the way it was done. Religion as the service of God, love for fellow men, even "good will," were ignored. John Buchan's famous words on the beheading of Charles I described their feelings admirably: "However the 'zealots,' 'dogmatists,' and 'hot gospellers' might approve . . . to all who had a care for the human decencies it seemed that a cruel wrong had been done."[22]

A tactic to be expected in such performances was the dropping of goodwillers in favor of tough laity. It was a shock for some of them to be used and then discarded. Even the two embarrassed members of the Royal Commission were eased aside without being consulted or informed on what the final steps would be. A condoling letter from Norman MacKenzie said he had "no information about the issues involved in the current situation," which was a sad admission for him to make.[23]

It was left to Rev. Dr. J.S. Bonnell, Chairman of the Royal Commission, to pronounce burial – an academic Nunc Dimittis:

"Prince Edward Islanders seem to have lost their nerve and the will to put up any kind of battle. It looks as if P.W.C. will be wiped out which will be a first-class disaster for education in the Maritime Provinces. It wouldn't surprise me if most of the students will go over to the mainland for their education and the government will find itself saddled with a sectarian university on its hands. Nobody in Prince Edward Island ever thinks of sending me clippings from the *Guardian* when some news item is published so I don't know what's going on there, but I suspect it bodes no good for P.W.C. It's a sad business."[24]

Following the dreams and commotions of Island education, other events reinforced the legacy of church politics:

No rumpus was allowed to stop the Roman Catholic Community College of Cape Breton from getting government-financed university status in 1982, when there were already thirteen universities and colleges in Nova Scotia alone, of which five had been Catholic and seven were in Halifax with no plans for union among any of them!

Twenty-five years after the 134 year-old Prince of Wales was sacrificed, Bishop MacEachern's "foundation for the future" of the Island ranked in the *Macleans* national assessment of Canadian universities below the standings of *all* the Atlantic universities that existed during the change of 1968, both sectarian and non-sectarian!

Recent official comments suggest planning post secondary facilities to suit the citizens.[25] This process should be reversed for a change. Islanders now need to adjust their values to the demanding requirements of modern education and employment. Their economic and political efforts and spiritual and cultural qualities will thrive if they exert initiative, become productive, and pay their own bills. The Island way of life needs more life in it.

The province lost two opportunities to get a splendid well-financed university. A third chance might succeed if churchmen back off, so education can serve the people in its own ways with high standards that the Island greatly needs. Religion in turn will have more scope if church politics are curtailed.

New challenges of old problems were evident in the budget speech of 1995 in the House of Commons. Its approach to federalism could make Canada a communitiy of communities with the Roman administration of Emperor Constantine and the features described in chapter 4. Island experience indicates that church politics in Canada could increase as government is dispersed, with clerical politicians secretly dominating in all dioceses and provinces, under episcopal potentates in Ottawa. Unity could then become monopoly control in token federalism without the public knowing it. The problem is not conflicting national and local juristictions, but the invasion of them by ecclesiastics, who in politics are eminently dispensable.

A recent article entitled "Requiem for Island" in the *Guardian* sounded the ultimate warning: "Paul Martin's budget speech, the state of the provincial legislature and the fixed link. . . . are major strides on the short road leading to the end of Prince Edward Island as a province. . . . The money market has replaced the electorate. It calls the shots . . . [and] is telling us something: Goodbye, P.E.I."[26] Other shots have been called by church politics, and the results tell the same message.

A modern Edict of Nantes may well be needed to prevent this dispersal and preserve civil rights, so democratic government and leadership will be strong enough in challenging times. Canada started with one and it worked (pp. 16-17). She should try it again.

The ghosts of Cardinal Richelieu and Father Joseph were no doubt pleased with these events, and agreeably astonished at Prince Edward Island being a so easily manipulated victim. They may even be dreaming of a similar conquest on a national scale, should Canadians not protect their democracy and religion against the ravage of church politics.

APPENDICES

A. Recommendations of the Citizens' Committee

B. Recommendations of the Royal Commission on Higher Education

C. Views of the "Study Group"

D. Resolution of the United Church Presbytery

E. About the Bishop's letter to his priests, December 12, 1966

APPENDIX A

Recommendations of the Citizens' Committee

As a result of this study this committee unanimously concludes:

1. That it is entirely feasible from educational, administrative, and financial viewpoints to proceed immediately with the proposal to elevate Prince of Wales College to the level of a degree granting institution.

2. That such a move is not only feasible, but highly desirable and even necessary for the welfare of our province and of our youth.

3. That the excellent academic standards of Prince of Wales College be maintained, and that the most effective way of maintaining these standards is to constitute Prince of Wales College as a separate entity.

4. That the only desirable and effective way to accomplish this purpose would be to constitute Prince of Wales College as a non-sectarian, publicly owned institution, open to all.

5. That such a move would not constitute a major additional drain on our Provincial Treasury.

6. That for purposes of academic stature, efficient administration, and adequate financing for such an institution, Prince of Wales College, like other provincially owned colleges, be responsible to an autonomous Board of Governors.

7. That the practice of following the standards for courses as set by McGill University and Dalhousie University be continued.

8. That, at least initially, efforts be confined to granting degrees in only the liberal arts, science, and education.

9. That diploma courses be given in Agricultural Science, Fisheries, and Secretarial Science.

10. That the committee continue as an unofficial group of interested citizens, to work toward these objectives. That we make ourselves and our findings available to all parties, official and private, who are interested in this matter. And further that we invite all others to participate with us in this endeavour and to add their knowledge, advice, and support to our humble efforts.

This report was distributed by a volunteer committee chaired by Dr. Paul Cudmore, with the title "Report of a Citizens' Committee to Study the Feasibility of Prince of Wales College Becoming a Degree Granting Institution," July 1962.

APPENDIX B

Recommendations of the Royal Commission on Higher Education, January 20, 1965

1. St. Dunstan's and Prince of Wales "should attempt to achieve the maximum cooperation possible." (p. 21)

2. The Boards of Governors (of S.D.U. and P.W.C.) should study the feasibility of federation with a view to providing the highest quality of education for all students who can qualify. (p. 43)

3. Such cooperation will be the best possible preparation for some later form of federation, if this should be found desirable and feasible. (p. 21)

4. Obviously a genuine federation of two educational institutions can be successfully accomplished only as it is the expression of will and desire of all parties to the union and is free from any element of coercion. (p. 32)

5. The Prince of Wales College Act 1964 should be proclaimed at once; that its Board of Governors be appointed and that they proceed to provide for four years of college courses. (p. 42)

6. It is very important that a special basic grant be made to Prince of Wales College. . . . Initially this grant should contain (1) the budget that the college is now operating on, (2) a supplementary grant to enable it to develop from a two year to a four year institution, (3) a grant to enable the college to reconvert, renovate, repair, and redecorate the entire plant for university purposes. (p. 19)

APPENDIX C

Views of the "Study Group"

In Prince Edward Island this level of academic excellence can be attained only by having a single university.

The existence of two universities . . . has been determined solely by our attitudes towards our religious differences and the resultant inabilities to arrive at an effective compromise.

Frank admission, open acceptance, and free expression of religious differences can create that situation which makes possible a single university on P.E.I.

That religion, as expressed in academic courses and other campus activities, should be present in the University.

The question has been raised as to whether or not there might be conflict between the complete expression of academic freedom in placing books in this single library, and the "Index Prohibitorum" of the Roman Catholic Church. We are advised by those competent in such matters that such a conflict simply will not exist.*

. . . . we see in this a mechanism whereby the study of religion can become a truly meaningful component of the students' university experience . . . in which the Christian viewpoint of life can thrive and find meaningful expression.

We hold that, given a true understanding of academic freedom, a dedication to learning, and above all a Christian concern for our fellow men, that we can have a truly Christian University in this province.

Also implicit in the single administrative structure is the equal representation of the Catholic and Protestant faiths on the Board of Governors.

. . . . two appointments to the Board to be made by the Government, one each from slates of candidates recommended by the Ministerial Association and the Bishop of Charlottetown.

. . . . the university shall accept divine revelation as a true source of knowledge and as the highest source of truth in spiritual matters.

The University shall provide classroom facilities and opportunities . . . for all Christian communions.

The instructors of these courses shall be recommended by their communions.

Finally, we ask that all men of good will who are concerned primarily with the provision of the best possible system of university education in our province, join with us in pursuing this goal of a single university for our province.

These views were distributed in two pamphlets of a group co-chaired by M. N. Beck and J. H. Maloney, entitled "A Single University for Prince Edward Island," May 28, 1965, and "Religious Studies in University Education," March 10, 1967.

* *Book vetting by church people did exist at the very time the "study group" reported. Prince of Wales ordered its library books through the purchasing facilities of the provincial libraries, and certain allegedly "controversial" books were delayed or refused. At faculty request I had to intervene a few times and see to it that the orders were filled.*

APPENDIX D

Resolution of the United Church Presbytery

5 February 1965

Presbytery of Prince Edward Island
Hampton P.O., P.E.I.
Rev. Bryer R. Jones, B.A., B.D. Secretary

Dr. Frank MacKinnon, M.A., Ph.D., LL.D.
Principal of Prince of Wales College,
Charlottetown, Prince Edward Island.

Dear Dr. MacKinnon:

At a meeting of the Executive of the Presbytery of Prince Edward Island, held at Charlottetown, on Wednesday, February 24th, 1965, the matter of the work of the so-called Citizens' Committee on Education was discussed.

I have been instructed by the Executive to inform you, Sir, that the views expressed by the two ministers of The United Church of Canada, who are members of the Committee, are their own personal opinions, and do not represent the official position of the Presbytery on the question of university education here on Prince Edward Island. They are acting as individuals in this matter, and not as official representatives of the United Church of Canada.

The resolutions of the Presbytery recommending that degree-granting status be given to Prince of Wales College still stand, and are the only official statements made by the Presbytery on the matter of University education in this Province.

Yours very truly,

Bryer R. Jones

(NOTE: The Presbytery was referring to the study group, not the Citizens' Committee.)

APPENDIX E

About the Bishop's letter to his priests, December 12, 1966

The letter on the university question from Bishop Malcolm MacEachern to the priests of his diocese was in the church tradition of secrecy and lack of discussion. "It should be considered *confidential and not for publication. . . .*" wrote the Bishop, "We would not want the press to get a hold of it." Nevertheless, the letter was widely distributed. There should be copies in the P.W.C. files at U.P.E.I., and there is no doubt one in the Archives.

This document is in effect a presumptuous declaration by the Bishop that he was a court of compulsory appeal from all the public institutions of the province. It mattered not to him that consent for Prince of Wales' development had been given by the Board of Governors, the Citizens' Committee, the Royal Commission, the Cabinet, and the Legislature, despite vicious attacks by churchmen. And the Association of Universities and Colleges of Canada had admitted Prince of Wales to its membership. The only reason the College had not been so elevated decades before, like other similar institutions, was the perennial political obstruction by the Bishop's clerical and lay predecessors. And the Island had suffered acutely from the resulting lost opportunities like the Sir William Macdonald/McGill/Prince of Wales plan for which more than ample recognition and funds were available to the College.

J.P. Nicholson's letter (as summarized in chapter 7) illustrated the reasons for the Bishop's attack. One was the widely held opinion everywhere that "the rightful place of religion . . . is not in a public institution of higher education;" the religious heritage that has "withstood the test of time . . . stands on a firm foundation of complete separation of Church and State. . . . A single university in Prince Edward Island is certainly possible and indeed is desirable, so long as that university has absolutely no religious overtones or under-currents." Prince of Wales was never anti-religion, but was a victim of the countless "overtones" and "under-currents" which were disguised as religion, but were not religion, only church politics. Important and arguable as this subject was, churchmen labelled it bigoted and never allowed it to be openly discussed on the Island.

A second reason for the Bishop's attack was Prince of Wales' unmatched reputation on the Island that was widely recognized nationally. McGill, for example, had told the local premier of "the thorough preparation of the many excellent students" of the College who had gone there. Yet, wrote Mr. Nicholson, "It would seem that Prince of Wales College must be down-graded to St. Dunstan's University standards." This tactic the Bishop pursued with a pretentious arrogance that had no basis in fact. "P.W.C. is so far behind us" he wrote, "it will take years for Prince of Wales to acquire any kind of reputable standing, and S.D.U. must therefore take the initiative in representing the strongest voice in the field." That voice, one may presume, was the Bishop himself. Strange he did not think that once McGill invited Prince of Wales into a union with it, who was he to express such an opinion? And why did he not recall the description in the Learned-Sills Report of St. Dunstan's standards, and of its becoming a "university" with eight priests and a layman, and the situation three decades later with fourteen itinerant priests and six laymen, with the standards of Prince of Wales being much higher on both occasions (see p. 37)? One cannot politely call the Bishop's opinion a lie; but one can say that, if a lie was intended, the same words would express it well.

Even though the Bishop admits that "in fact S.D.U. is looked upon by all of us as a Catholic Church-related University – a church affiliated and even dominated institution," he rejected the separation of church and state out of hand. He declared with pontifical certainty that an "Institute of Christian Studies" should be provided to "safe-guard the Christian traditions." As earlier pages have indicated, "St. Dunstan's," he said, "must be the foundation on which the structure of higher education and adult education for the future is built." Where did he think the government, Prince of Wales, and the new university should stand? His words leave no room for their opinions.

These remarks are naïveté expressed in arrogant bluster. How could the Bishop make them and then complain that "all evidence points to the fact that there will be no serious attempt at cooperation with St. Dunstan's on the part of Prince of Wales?" There was no reason, academic, financial, or otherwise, why Prince of Wales should attempt such cooperation in view of the much lower standards at S.D.U., the policies of political authoritarianism following decades of assault by churchmen, and the antics recently displayed in the legislative caucus.

Prince of Wales as a reputable public institution could hardly be expected to agree with another episcopal statement. "Confronted as we are with practical agnosticism and scepticism among the youth – especially among the most intellectual of them – it is becoming of greater importance that the talents of the clergy within the university be used in the most effective manner. . . . Our Diocese . . . has a right to turn to the University for aid in its attempts to adjust to its new work in the light of the various documents of Vatican Council II." Confronted with practical agnosticism and scepticism? especially among the most intellectual? the talents of the clergy within the university be used? aid in the light of Vatican Council II? These are not responsibilities of a public university. The wording suggests church politics, not religion, as well as dominating church control over education. The assessment of separate schools in chapter 4 applies.

"If we continue as we are," wrote the Bishop, "then there is no doubt that neither P.W.C. nor S.D.U. will be able to offer students the kind of program which will be necessary at the undergraduate level within the next ten years." He could of course speak for S.D.U. But for Prince of Wales he was unwilling to admit that the College had already been operating the necessary program and had the required plans, standards, personnel, and recognition, despite the opposition of his church.

The Bishop's attitude to finance was the old idea that whatever money was spent on a public college had to be duplicated for the church one, otherwise the church should prevent the public one from getting what it needed and deserved from either public or private sources. This policy had been evident throughout the years every time Prince of Wales had an opportunity or presented a budget. Sir William Macdonald's assurance of university financing for Prince of Wales was conveniently forgotten, as the church dunned the government for money. And the government and public were misinformed when told that money would be saved with one university rather than two. As I have noted, consultants told the P.W.C. Board of Governors, which in turn told the government and the press, that the combination would be much more costly because of the internal politics, the frustrating inefficiency, the difficulty of getting things done because of "compromise which pleases no-one and frustrates everyone with a resulting mediocrity which produces second or third rate education." As for "the Island cannot afford it" argument, the provincial government pays little or nothing for post-secondary education. The federal government bears the load.

Never mind these arguments, we will not discuss or answer them, our view must prevail: this was the approach of the Bishop and his followers. Force was therefore their tactic. "Our move," the Bishop wrote, "would force P.W.C. into some kind of real and sincere cooperation [how does one force real and sincere cooperation?], such as cross appointments to faculty . . . since there would be no justification in not entering into some form of union with us, to the academic advantage of students." On the contrary, there was ample justification. The cooperating was to be on Prince of Wales' part only. The Royal Commission had warned against coercion. The church had never encouraged "cooperation with," only "domination by," and in practice on the Island it was the Bishop's wishes that prevailed whenever the government was weak. The Colleges, to note the example, had already had three cross-appointments and the instructors had to be Catholic. And the "academic advantage to students" of the combination of church and state was a mirage for obvious reasons. The whole problem and all these facts were well illustrated when, as the last chapter describes, the church attempted to gain complete control of the new university in July 1969.

Prince of Wales and Island education were not alone in suffering from the Bishop's church politics. Weak government and the public interest were assaulted and easily overcome. The main victim was religion.

Endnotes

Chapter 1. Introduction: The Setting

1. David Jenkins (Bishop of Durham), *Manchester Guardian Weekly*, 15 November 1987.
2. Quote from Miss Marple in Agatha Christie's *The Companion*.
3. *Time* Magazine, 15 March 1993, 2.
4. Maggie Siggins. *Revenge of the Land* (Toronto: McClelland & Stewart, 1991), ix-x.
5. James Gray. *The Roar of the Twenties* (Toronto: Macmillan, 1982), 2.
6. *Canadian Historical Review.* June 1977.

Chapter 2. Background: From Paris to Charlottetown

1. Conrad Black, *A Life in Progress* (Toronto: KeyPorter, 1993), 9.
2. Canadian Press [CP], 1 December 1985.
3. Stephen Leacock, *Canada and the Foundation of its Future* (Montreal: Seagram, 1941), 55.
4. J.M.S. Careless, *Canada: A Story of Challenge* (Toronto: Macmillan, 1986), 64-65.
5. See note 2.
6. Aldous Huxley, *Grey Eminence* (Cleveland: World Publishing, 1952), 24.
7. *Ibid.*, 193.
8. *Ibid.*, 203.
9. *Charlottetown Guardian*, 23 April 1984. The works of Maritime authors Thomas H. Raddall and H.A. Cody have accounts of LeLoutre's activities in the troubles of the region.
10. *Macleans*, 30 April 1990. Another apppraisal is in Peter Ustinov's *Dear Me* (London: Penguin, 1977), 164.
11. CP Vancouver, 12 December 1992; *Guardian*, 10 August 1994.
12. *Globe and Mail*, 29 August 1992.
13. Helmut de Terra, *Humboldt* (New York: Knopf, 1955), 117. Other well known treatments of this subject are Alan Moorhead's *The Fatal Impact* (New York: Harper, 1966); and R.C. Suggs' *The Hidden World of Polynesia* (Toronto: Mentor, 1962).
14. J.V. Langmead Casserly, *The Retreat from Christianity in the Modern World* (London: Longmans Green, 1952), 11. See also my *Postures and Politics* (Toronto: University of Toronto Press, 1973), ch. 10 and 11.

15. Frank G. Slaughter, *Constantine. Pathway of Faith Series* (New York: Richmond Hill, 1967), 1: 301, 349.
16. Edward Gibbon, *The Decline and Fall of the Roman Empire* (New York: Dell, 1963), 220.

Chapter 3. Politics and the Colleges

1. For a detailed description see my *The Government of Prince Edward Island* (Toronto: University of Toronto Press, 1951) and my "Big Engine, Little Body" in *Canadian Provincial Politics*, 2nd ed. Martin Robin, ed. (Toronto: Prentice-Hall, 1978), 222-248.
2. J.M. Bumsted, *Land Settlement, and Politics on Eighteenth-Century Prince Edward Island* (Kingston, Montreal: McGill-Queens University Press, 1987), 193.
3. For examples of the difficulties, see *P.E.I. Assembly Debates* from 1830 to 1838, and letters in the Public Archives of Canada, P.E.I., A series, vol. 54-2 and vol. 57.
4. *Assembly Debates*, 1861,12.
5. 24 Victoria 1861, 17.
6. Karen Kearney, *Guardian*, 15 April 1992.
7. G. Edward MacDonald, *The History of St. Dunstan's University 1855-1956* (Charlottetown: Board of Govenors, S.D.U. & P.E.I. Museum and Heritage Foundation, 1989).
8. *Ibid.*
9. *Ibid.*, 202, 269, 301.
10. *Ibid.*, 291.
11. They became the University of British Columbia, University of Victoria, University of Guelph, and Macdonald College respectively.
12. Premier Peters to McGill University Registrar, 17 April 1907. Copies of these letters should be in the P.W.C. files at U.P.E.I.
13. P.W.C. files, 13 Sept. 1906.
14. *Ibid.*, 21 Sept. 1906.
15. *Ibid.*, 24 Sept. 1906.
16. *Ibid.*, 17 Nov. 1906.
17. *Ibid.*, 22 Nov. 1906.
18. *Ibid.*, 28 Jan. 1907.
19. *Ibid.*, 5 April 1907.
20. Sir James Duff and R.O. Berdahl, *University Government in Canada* (Toronto: University of Toronto Press, 1966), 43.
21. MacDonald, *History of St. Dunstan's*, 267-8.
22. *Ibid.*, 269.

23. William S. Learned and Kenneth C.M. Sills, *Education in the Maritime Provinces of Canada* (New York: Carnegie Foundation, 1922).

24. *Ibid.*, 27, 48.

25. *Ibid.*

Chapter 4. Community of Communities

1. Gérard Pelletier, *Years of Impatience* (Toronto: Methuen, 1984), 51.

2. *Ibid.*, 65-66.

3. *Globe and Mail*, 2 April 1993.

4. *Ibid.*, 15 March 1989.

5. *Ibid.*, 20 July 1992.

6. *Calgary Herald*, 25 June 1992.

7. *Globe and Mail*, 27 May 1992.

8. Ibid., 13 March 1989.

9. CP Toronto, 28 December 1985.

10. *Ibid.*

11. *Globe and Mail*, 13 March 1989.

12. American Press [AP] Santo Domingo, 15 October 1992.

13. *National Catholic Reporter*, 26 April 1989.

14. *Ibid.*

15. *Ibid.*

16. CP Winnipeg, 21 January 1993.

17. *Globe and Mail*, 12 March 1993.

18. *Globe and Mail*, 25 and 26 April 1989.

19. London Free Press, 27 January 1967.

20. Franklin Sonn, Rector of Peninsula Technikon, and president of the Union of Teachers' Associations of South Africa, *Johannesburg Star*, 18 June 1985.

21. *Globe and Mail*, 4 October 1994.

22. *Macleans*, 18 January 1988.

23. Clair Hoy, *Bill Davis* (Toronto: Methuen, 1985), 264-5.

24. *Ibid.*

25. *Globe and Mail*, 8 March, 1988.

26. CP Toronto, 26 April 1985.

27. H.L. Mencken, *Prejudices* (New York: Vantage, 1958), 29, 123.

28. John Buchan, *Cromwell* (London: Sphere, 1971), 439.

29. Walter Bagehot, *Physics and Politics* (Boston: Beacon, 1956), 56, 119-120.

30. Conrad Black, *A Life in Progress*, 301.

31. Marnie Jackson, *Destinations Magazine,* April 1988, 26.
32. *Globe and Mail,* 29 April 1986.

Chapter 5. To Prince of Wales College

1. Thomas H. Raddall, *In My Time* (Toronto: McClelland and Stewart, 1976), 242.
2. *Massey Papers Diary,* 21 & 25 January 1950.
3. Garth Jenkins, *Guardian,* 26 November 1991.
4. *Globe and Mail,* 7 September 1992.
5. Southam News Dispatch, 6 December 1987.
6. *Ibid.*
7. *Guardian,* 20 February 1981.
8. A detailed discussion of this controversial issue is in my *The Politics of Education* (Toronto: University of Toronto Press, 1961).
9. Learned and Sills, *Education in the Maritime Provinces.*

Chapter 6. Church Politics

1. *Calgary Herald,* 10 December 1987.
2. *Globe and Mail,* 18 May 1992.
3. CP Toronto, 31 October 1992.
4. Clifford Longley, religious reporter for *The Times* (London), 7 January 1985.
5. *Time,* 18 May 1992.
6. *Globe and Mail,* 9 November 1984.
7. *Guardian,* 4 April 1966.
8. Harold Harwood, "Divine Intervention," *Saturday Night,* October 1989.
9. Harry Golden, *For 2 Cents Plain* (Montreal: Perma Books, 1960), 1981.
10. Sir Charles Petrie, *The Victorians* (London: Eyre and Spottiswoode, 1960), 230.
11. Elizabeth Longford, *Victoria RI* (London: Wiedenfeld and Nicholson, 1964), 548.
12. Times-Post Service, 12 November 1988.
13. AP Vatican City, 31 May 1986.
14. John Cooney, *The American Pope: The Life and Times of Francis Cardinal Spellman* (New York: Times Books, 1984), 303.
15. Charles Lynch, *Race for the Rose* (Toronto: Methuen, 1984), 22; *Calgary Herald,* 25 February 1984.
16. *Globe and Mail,* 23 December 1994.
17. See p. 116, Esther Deslisle's quote (chapter 8, note 15).

18. Fritz Pannehock, *Globe and Mail*, 11 July 1992.
19. Herb Dickieson, *Guardian*, 8 December 1993 and 9 December 1994.
20. L.G. Dewar, *Prescription for a Full Life* (Summerside, P.E.I.: Williams and Crue, 1993), 258-267.
21. For an early discussion on appointing Catholic staff to Prince of Wales, see P.E.I. *The Examiner*, 30 November 1869 and *The Herald*, 1 September 1868.
22. *Legislative Assembly Debates* P.E.I., 17 March 1964.
23. See also Professor H.H.J. Nesbit of Carleton cited on the subject by Cheryl Lloyd in Carelton's alumni magazine, 1991.
24. See series of letters in *Guardian* and *Patriot*, November and December 1951. On this subject see also *Public Servant: The Memoirs of Sir Joseph Pope* (Toronto: Oxford Press, 1960).
25. *Globe and Mail*, 29 January 1932. Montreal Free Press, 26 June 1937; and D'Arcy Marsh, *The Tragedy of Henry Thornton*, (Toronto: Macmillan, 1935).
26. He is reported in the *Patriot*, 8 April 1952; 30 March 1954; 20 May 1952; 9 February 1954; 11, 12, 15, 18, 19, 25, 26, 31 March and 1, 2, 5, 8, 10 April 1954. In the *Guardian*, 29, 30, January 1954; 3, 5, 6, 8, 9, 10, 17, 18, 22, 24 February 1954; 2, 8, 9, 10, 12, 15, 30, 31 March 1954. Senator Walter Jones also replied to Dr. Macmillan in *Patriot* on 19 March 1954, two weeks before his death.
27. *Patriot*, 15 March 1954.
28. My comments are to be found in *Patriot*, 30 May 1952; 25, 26 March 1954; *Guardian*, 30 January 1954; 8, 25, 26 March 1954.
29. On attempted secrecy in the proceedings see the *Patriot*, 2 April 1954.
30. *Patriot*, 2 April 1954.
31. *Patriot*, 25 March 1954, 2 April 1954.
32. *Guardian*, 10 April 1954.
33. M.A. Boswell, *Guardian*, 5 April 1954.
34. *Patriot*, 25 March 1954.
35. John B. McNair to A.W. Trueman, 24 April 1950.

Chapter 7. The March of Folly

1. For details see my *Honour the Founders, Enjoy the Arts*, published by the Confederation Centre, P.E.I., 1990.
2. *Time*, 22 March 1982.
3. *Time*, 16 December 1991.
4. Will and Ariel Durant, *The Age of Voltaire* (New York: Simon and Schuster, 1965), 119.

5. *Ibid.*, 152 -3.

6. *Macleans*, 2 January 1989.

7. Scarth Macdonnell, *The Striving for Unity*, a published address to the Presbytery of Ottawa, 14 April 1964.

8. Newspaper report, *The Square Deal*, Montague, April 1971.

9. Paul Johnson, *Pope John Paul II and the Catholic Restoration* (London: Weidenfeld, 1982; Paul Hebblethwaite, *Manchester Guardian*, 14 March 1982.

10. Rev. John Long, Pontifical Russian College, Rome: Ray Mosely, *Chicago Tribune* printed in the *Calgary Herald*, 21 November 1992.

11. *Globe and Mail*, 7 October 1986.

12. Mike Leary, *Calgary Herald*, 26 Aug. 1990 (Knight-Ridder newspapers).

13. Barbara Tuchman, *The March of Folly* (New York: Ballantine, 1984), 4, 5, 33.

14. *Ibid.*, 23.

15. *Guardian*, 8 August 1991.

16. Murray G. Ross, *New Universities in the Modern World* (Toronto: MacMillan, 1966), 183; chapters 5 and 11.

17. J.P. Nicholson to Frank MacKinnon, 17 February 1965. A copy of this long and interesting letter is to be found in the Public Archives of Prince Edward Island, Charlottetown.

18. Lewis H. Thomas, ed., *The Making of a Socialist: The Recollections of T.C. Douglas* (Edmonton: University of Alberta Press, 1982), 82, 185.

19. L. George Dewar, *Prescription for a Full Life* (Summerside, P.E.I.: Williams and Crue, 1993), 183.

20. *Ibid.*, 185.

21. *Guardian*, 20 March 1964; *Prince of Wales College Times*, 23 March 1964.

22. *Guardian*, 10 March 1992.

23. I asked Justice Darby to put what happened on paper. His letter is in the Public Archives of Prince Edward Island, Charlottetown.

24. Dewar, *Prescription for a Full Life*, 187.

25. *Ibid.*

26. *Globe and Mail*, 22 March 1967.

Chapter 8. The Going Down of the Sun

1. One such source book is Werner Rings, *Life with the Enemy: Collaboration and Resistance in Hitler's Europe, 1929 - 1945* (New York: Doubleday, 1982), 8.

2. Merle Miller, *Plain Speaking: An Oral Biography of Harry S. Truman* (New York: Berkley,1974), 254.

3. *Guardian,* 5 November 1966.

4. See former President Peter Meinke of the University of Prince Edward Island, *Guardian,* 16 February 1985.

5. I have described these affairs in the *Canadian Annual Review,* vols. 1963 to 1975.

6. P.B. Waite, *Lord of Point Grey* (Vancouver: U.B.C. Press, 1987), 214-215.

7. *Ibid.,* 198. A similar example of MacKenzie's approach, also in 1966, is in J.W. Pickerskill's memoirs about the transportation strike of 1966, *Seeing Canada Whole* (Ontario: Fitzhenry and Whiteside, 1994), 741.

8. Millar MacLure to Frank MacKinnon, 29 May 1968.

9. *Guardian,* 8 and 20 April 1968; and *Patriot,* 22 April 1968.

10. Minutes of a closed session of the Board of Governors, 28 July 1969.

11. *Cadre,* 25 November 1970.

12. *Globe and Mail,* 19 May 1994.

13. *Ibid.*

14. Don Jamieson, *No Place for Fools* (St. Johns, NF: Breakwater, 1989), Reviewed in *Saturday Night,* October 1989.

15. Esther Delisle, *The Traitor and the Jew* (Montreal: Robert Davies, 1993). Reviewed in *Globe and Mail,* 3 July 1993.

16. *Globe and Mail,* 9 June 1994; 23 November 1994.

17. *Calgary Herald,* 14 June 1995.

18. *Globe and Mail,* 7 and 9 June, 1994.

19. William Johnson, *A Canadian Myth: Quebec Between Canada and the Illusion of Utopia* (Montreal: Robert Davies Publishing, 1994), 14, 42, 404, 406.

20. *Guardian,* 2 September 1993.

21. T.M. Lothian to Frank MacKinnon, 8 October 1969.

22. John Buchan, *Cromwell* (London: Sphere Books, 1971), 318.

23. N.A.M. MacKenzie to Frank MacKinnon, 2 May 1968.

24. J.S. Bonnell to Frank MacKinnon, 13 November 1968. A copy of this letter is in the Public Archives of Prince Edward Island, Charlottetown.

25. *Globe and Mail,* 18 Oct. 1994, 25 Nov. 1994, 19 and 21 Jan., 8 and 21 Feb. 1995.

26. Martin Dorrell, In this Corner, *Guardian,* 11 March 1995.

Index

The Author

Frank MacKinnon is Professor Emeritus of Political Science, University of Calgary, and former Principal of Prince of Wales College, Charlottetown. A graduate of McGill University and the University of Toronto, he is author of many articles and seven books. He was an original member of the Canada Council, President of the Atlantic Provinces Economic Council, President of the Institute of Public Administration of Canada, and winner of the Canada Council Medal and the Govenor General's Literary Award for Non-Fiction. He is an Officer of the Order of Canada.

Acknowledgements

The author wishes to thank Dr. Roger Gibbins, head of the Department of Political Science, University of Calgary, for his help as the publication date neared, and the department's efficient Valerie Snowdon who prepared the manuscript and disc. As one who has great respect for book editors, I thank Tara Gregg of Detselig Enterprises, Calgary for her careful work and helpful cooperation. Above all, my wife Daphne has supported me with her usual encouragement as another book dominated at our house.